Feeling Right
When Things
Go Wrong

Bill Borcherdt, ACSW, BCD
Board Certified Diplomate
in Clinical Social Work

Professional Resource Press
Sarasota, Florida

Published by Professional Resource Press
(An imprint of Professional Resource Exchange, Inc.)
Post Office Box 15560
Sarasota, FL 34277-1560

The copy editor for this book was Patricia Rockwood, the managing editor was Debra Fink, the production coordinator was Laurie Girsch, and the cover was created by Jami S. Stinnet.

Library of Congress Cataloging-in-Publication Data

Borcherdt, Bill.
    Feeling right when things go wrong / Bill Borcherdt.
       p.   cm.
    Includes bibliographical references.
    ISBN 1-56887-036-1 (alk. paper)
    1. Rational-emotive psychotherapy. I. Title.
RC489.R3B667   1998
616.89'14--dc21
                                    98-35775
                                      CIP

Dedication

*To my once-in-a-lifetime friend
Dick Nooe,
an extraordinary human being.*

Other books by Bill Borcherdt
Available from
Professional Resource Press
P.O. Box 15560
Sarasota, FL 34277-1560
(800) 443-3364

Think Straight! Feel Great!
21 Guides to Emotional Self-Control

You Can Control Your Feelings!
24 Guides to Emotional Well-Being

Head Over Heart in Love:
25 Guides to Rational Passion

Table of Contents

Introduction

Humans guide their lives by their ideas. They bring to their circumstances, emotions, and behavior values that represent what life means for them. They then make decisions based on their value conclusions. The applied philosophy of rational emotive behavior therapy (REBT) quickly and efficiently makes people aware of their belief system, subjects it to close examination, and in active collaboration with the client determines whether those views do service to the individual's emotional well-being. It teaches clients to identify and rip up distorted thinking and replace it with ideas more comparable with mental health.

REBT was originated in 1955 by Albert Ellis, PhD. From the outset, his teaching identified a scientific method of thinking that intervenes in human thought in a way that allows its students to take much pressure off themselves and their relationships with others. REBT questions much psychotherapeutic wisdom about human thought, emotion, and behavior. Those who study REBT's principles and concepts often find that they are able, frequently in a short period of time, to use its logic and reason to help themselves to feel more the way they want to feel and less the way they don't want to feel - to better service their emotional well-being. Dr. Ellis is currently the President of the Albert Ellis Institute for Rational Emotive Behavior Therapy in New York City, which serves as the focal point for teaching REBT methods. There are also nationally and internationally based rational emotive behavior centers. REBT's cognitive, emotive, and behavioral principles are practiced by thousands of therapists all over the globe, a good number of whom were trained by Dr. Ellis and his Institute staff. Readers interested in receiving the Institute's semiannual brochure describing the various educational and training seminars and psychoeducational materials (e.g., books, pamphlets, posters, audio- and videotapes, etc.) can request one by writing the Institute at 45 East 65th Street, New York, NY 10021.

Philosophy can be defined as "that which gives meaning to life." Because REBT teaches the tact and tactics of becoming your own best philosopher, it is very depth centered. It zeroes in on the head and heart of what makes people tick and click. One thing that REBT is *not* very good at is confirming what you already believe by way of conventional wisdom. It consistently and persistently tries to create a profound values upheaval so that you can back up and start over again armed with a different worldview that will better your emotional self-interest. It takes dead aim at the common personal, family, and social values that are at the center of emotional disturbances. It roots for you as the home team to win out over the visiting disturbance. It does this by providing the psychological technology that can be used to realign your thinking in a less conventional and commercialized but healthier manner.

Rational emotive behavior therapy teachings include the following philosophic references. Acquiring and practicing these foundations allows students of REBT to approach life in a manner more befitting emotional health.

1. *Philosophy of fallibility.* Humans are by nature remarkably imperfect and are encouraged not to define themselves by their shortcomings.

2. *Philosophy of variability.* Humans are not only different from one another, but also differ within themselves by way of thoughts, feelings, and involuntary biochemical sensations. These differences frequently occur spontaneously, often for no special reason, and are best accepted rather than protested against.

3. *Philosophy of nonreciprocation.* REBT teaches that there is no law of the universe that says others have to do unto us as we do unto them. Although it is nice when others treat us like we kindly treat them, such returns on our emotional investments are not necessities.

4. *Philosophy of sustained effort.* The persistence factor is best not underestimated. Getting behind yourself and pushing is habit forming and has a life of its own. Consistently going to bat on behalf of yourself strengthens emotional stamina while increasing the chances of success.

5. *Philosophy of interdependence.* Humans do best when they do not try to be islands unto themselves. Nor would it be well to make themselves endlessly dependent on their social group. Rotation and balance between you, me, and us is the socially advisable ideal.

6. *Philosophy of parity.* Everyone is in life together and no one person is any better than another. There are no good or bad persons, only individuals who do good and bad things. REBT goes out of its way not to take a "self and other" rating stance in describing individuals in relationship to their behavior.

7. *Philosophy of self-interest.* REBT suggests that you put yourself first and keep others a close second to promote the give-and-take that is compatible with harmonious social living.

8. *Philosophy of nonavoidance.* The best way to change an irrational belief is to act against it. Repeated exposure to the object or person of concern will likely reduce your exaggerated belief system and dramatic feelings about the matter.

9. *Philosophy of preferential disputation.* REBT recommends that you dispute your irrational beliefs about your difficult life situation *before* you try to change it. This way you will upset yourself less about the problem and be better able to cope with it if it can't be changed.

10. *Philosophy of self-permissiveness.* The essence of good problem solving is to give yourself some emotional slack; to lighten up on yourself rather than tighten up. Permitting yourself an emotional breath of fresh air has value apart from outside changes that you may be able to accomplish.

11. *Philosophy of challenge.* Persistence against odds will frequently pay off. Accepting the challenge of marching to the tune of your own drummer by thinking and acting rationally in an irrational world is outlined in REBT principles.

12. *Philosophy of long-range pleasure.* Adopting a long-range view of life, by making short-run sacrifices for long-run gains and accepting present pain for future gain, is at the center of rational ideals.

13. *Philosophy of force.* Most of life's advantages are likely to require force and vigor if they are to be gained. Just as people very strongly tell themselves irrational ideas that cause emotional disturbance, it's best that they instruct themselves - without a "Pollyannaish" attitude - in countering rational ideas that have more emotional promise.

14. *Philosophy of vital absorption.* Happiness is a fleeting thing. It comes and goes in large part by how well you are able to control for your wants. Vital absorption in a selected project or cause that structures large amounts of your time can be more accessible by way of human meaning.

15. *Philosophy of self-empowerment.* Individuals are capable of emotional self-reliance with or without the support of their family or social system.

16. *Philosophy of dual beliefs.* All irrational ideas start with a rational component. This sensible beginning comes in the form of a stated preference, wish, or want (e.g., "I wish things were different"). REBT tries to get people to hold firm to these desires, as striving for what one wants gives meaning to life. It is when these hopes are blocked and the individual magnifies preferences into demands that emotional disturbance erupts (e.g., "I wish things to be different, therefore they have to be different"). By giving up the demand component of the belief, emotional upset is interrupted.

17. *Philosophy of comfort.* One of the most valuable things people can learn is a healthy perspective to their discomfort. Worshipping the avoidance of it will lead to an avoidant lifestyle. Accepting rather than intimidating oneself about discomfort will promote an expanded lifestyle. Humans are in the world to experience the world, which includes a fair amount of discomfort.

18. *Philosophy of containment.* To perfectionistically try to eliminate unwanted emotions would not be rational. To seek to lessen their frequency, intensity, and duration while accepting yourself with your emotional cavities will help to set boundaries on them.

19. *Philosophy of tolerance.* Convincing yourself that you can stand what you don't like allows you to be well grounded in curtailing your frustrations.

20. *Philosophy of grace and forgiveness.* To damn or condemn a human (including yourself) is immoral and encourages a continuation of problems.

21. *Philosophy of approval.* Much of what is called anxiety is being overly concerned about what others might think of you. Understanding that you are not at the mercy of others' opinions of you better lubricates your relationships with them.

22. *Philosophy of respect for human limits.* Acknowledging that the sky is not the limit by way of human potential

reduces the frustration that comes from not knowing what to realistically expect from self and others.

23. *Philosophy of acceptance.* Undamning acceptance of self, others, and life is a fundamental premise of rational living.

24. *Philosophy of human contradiction.* Humans routinely don't practice what they preach. Pledging to more consistently practice affirmed ideals, while not condemning oneself for not hitting the bull's-eye, is suggested.

25. *Philosophy of antiawfulizing or antiexaggerating.* A cornerstone of emotional well-being is not dramatizing the significance of disappointment.

26. *Philosophy of uncertainty.* Accepting the deficiencies of surety, certainty, and orderliness in this world permits less confusion about and more enjoyment of what it does offer.

27. *Philosophy of antipamperingness.* Running from pain increases suffering. Taking the long, easy way rather than the short, hard way is standard operating procedure in rational thinking.

28. *Philosophy of antiindulgence of feelings.* REBT does not put extraordinary emphasis on touching base with feelings and then unreflectively expressing them. Rather, it prefers that the thoughts that propelled the feelings be examined for being fact and helpful or fiction and harmful.

29. *Philosophy of "upset-ability."* Humans are born with the ability to emotionally upset themselves. REBT takes a dim view of the idea that family of origin or other intrusive background factors are crucial in understanding how humans disturb themselves.

30. *Philosophy of nonpresumptuousness.* REBT does not presume that because you experience feelings in a situation, the circumstances caused the feelings. Nor does it presume that if you have a problem you wish to solve, you must solve it. Instead, it is the faulty thoughts that you take on in the circumstances that cause unwanted

feelings and warrant correction. Furthermore, people can learn to more peacefully coexist with their emotional tumors rather than put undue pressure on themselves to eliminate them.

31. *Philosophy of self-encouragement.* People can get by without outside reinforcement by reinforcing themselves with heavy doses of encouraging self-talk.

32. *Philosophy of anticomplacency.* Mental health and happiness is not a place that you get to and in which you then, once and for all, remain. Nothing works but working; keep on working to gain and remain in a healthier state of mind.

This, then, is a book about rational emotive behavior therapy's applied philosophical principles. REBT uses illustrations from different areas of life to demonstrate a point. Each of these philosophies is woven into the content of the 30 rational living guides to follow. Each guide is different, but the rational points made in each are consistent with REBT theory and practice.

Perhaps more than any other problem-solving approach, REBT holds you accountable for your emotions. Accepting this higher level of responsibility holds good promise for putting yourself more in the driver's seat to be your own best problem-solving philosopher. Unfortunately, due to natural tendencies to overreact and to take disappointments personally, humans approach their life circumstances with philosophies that reek with demands in the form of "have to"s. Consequently, they put much pressure on themselves and their relationships with others and stumble through their problem-solving efforts. The core trinity of emotional disturbances that REBT tries to dismantle are:

- "I have to be perfect."
- "Others have to treat me perfectly."
- "Life has to be perfectly easy."

In applying REBT's scientific principles, it follows that activating events or happenings at point "A" don't cause emotional consequences or feelings at point "C." Rather, it is one's belief system or philosophy about the happening (at point "B") that creates feelings. Therefore, by debating or disputing your original ideas in the service of a different way of thinking at point "D," you can bring on more effective emotional and behavioral results at "E."

To illustrate:

A →	B →	C →	D →	E
You perform less than perfect.	"I have to do better."	Stress, Tension, Anxiety	"I hope to do better, but my life doesn't depend on it."	Less stress and tension; concerned but not consumed about your performances.
Others treat you less than perfectly.	"Others have to treat me better."	Fear, Anger	"I wish significant others would treat me better, but my life doesn't depend on it."	Regret, Displeasure
Life's hassles and difficulties reappear.	"Life has to be easier than it often is, and I have to be able to make it so when it isn't."	Anguish, High Frustration	"It would be nice if life were easier, but it's not the end of the world when it isn't."	Disappointment

Use principles of rational living to form values that add depth and flexibility to your life's views. First, bring out your potential to make what is bad, okay, by undisturbing yourself. Then, make what is okay, better, by using your clearheadedness to more freely choose philosophies that contribute to feelings that reflect the "E" in REBT: more *excitement*, *energy*, and *enjoyment* in and about life.

Bill Borcherdt, ACSW, BCD
August, 1998

Feeling Right When Things Go Wrong

Emotional Applesauce
As Disturbance:
When Preference and Demand
Are Made to Run Together

This guide is about distinctive ideas that create distinctive emotions. More exactly, it reports on where emotional sanity leaves off and emotional disturbance begins. Separating preferences, wishes, and wants from demands and commands sheds much light on the human emotional condition. Emotions don't run together like most people think. Just as peaches can be distinguished from pears, or fact from fiction, feelings too can be sorted out in a way that highlights their individual existence. The purpose of fine tuning the anatomy of emotions is to use this understanding to better control your feelings. In that humans have feelings about everything they do, what could be a more significant area of study and a better investment of your resources?

Having values and desires and wanting to realize them provides meaning and substance to life. Ambitions make the world go around. Without strong personal preferences and likes, life would become monotonous. This is a well and good part of the human condition. It is when these wishes are amplified into demands (i.e., "Because something that I want is good, I have to have it") that emotional disturbance is created.

This fine dividing line between wanting a good thing that may be within your grasp and dictating that you have to have it makes a major difference as to the quality of one's personal emotional experience. The split second you tell yourself that you have to have what you desire is the moment you create emotional disturbance. This disturbance can be interrupted by putting the brakes on your demands and switching back to your original preferences.

The following are examples of helpful rational preferences multiplied into unhelpful, irrational demands and the contrasted feelings each produces.

RATIONAL PREFERENCES	IRRATIONAL DEMANDS
1. "I would like to know tomorrow's outcome so that I could better prepare for it, and I'm concerned that I don't." (Concern, Wonder)	"I have to know what is going to happen next, because if I don't, I won't be able to brace myself for the worst possible occurrence, which would be awful - if not the living end." (Worry, Fear)
2. "I would like to feel more comfortable while involved in my new project, because then I will be able to concentrate and perform better and enjoy it more." (Hopefulness, Alertness)	"I have to feel more comfortable while involved in my projects, because I can't stand feeling out of sorts, I can't concentrate as well when I feel nervous, and I am more likely to fail due to my lack of focus - and any or all of these negative outcomes would be awfully demeaning and discrediting." (Discomfort, Anxiety, Fear, Worry)
3. "I have a decided preference for gaining the acceptance and approval of my social group, because life without it would be less delightful and more inconvenient." (Apprehension, Alertness)	"I need the liking of my associates, and not meeting these requirements would be terrible and terribly degrading." (Worry, Depression, Disapproval, Anxiety)
4. "I want to perform and achieve well because of the advantages such success will supply; if not, I will feel keenly disappointed when I come up short in my hard-working efforts to	"I've got to be successful at whatever I put a lot of effort into because I need the advantages I find desirable; in addition, failure is discrediting, and I couldn't tolerate feeling any more

RATIONAL PREFERENCES *(Cont'd)*	IRRATIONAL DEMANDS *(Cont'd)*
accomplish my ends." (Concern, Sense of Anticipation and Participation, Self-Confidence)	inferior than I already do." (Performance Anxiety, Worry, Nervousness)
5. "Because I find warmth and closeness to be very much to my liking, I hope to establish a love bond with the person who is presently the most significant person in my life; missing my designated love boat would certainly be sad and regretful." (Apprehension, Concern)	"I must attach to my loved one, because being able to do so will make my world go around, and not being able to do so will cause me to be more dizzy and depressed than I already am." (Fear, Self-Downing)
6. "I wish there were an easier, quicker, more accessible way to accomplish my goals; the fact that there apparently isn't is disappointing and regretful." (Displeased)	"Life has to be easier than it oftentimes is, and I have to make it so when it unbearably and intolerably isn't. Not being able to accomplish this gets me lower than a snake's belly." (Anguish)
7. "I have a keen wish to avoid conflict with others most of the time, because I usually have better things to do than debate with those whose values can be contrasted with mine." (Apprehension)	"I have to avoid conflict at all costs, because such rocking of the boat makes me seasick to the point that is undeniably beyond reality." (Fear, Anxiety, Nervousness)
8. "I would like my associates to treat me kindly and gently like I treat them, and I certainly don't appreciate it when they don't; after all, life is more enjoyable when all concerned treat one another exceedingly pleasantly and decently." (Annoyance, Irritation)	"Others have to treat me well, especially if I make it a point to make myself consistently favorably disposed toward them; when such ideal provisions are overlooked, the overlooker is to be condemned and blasted as a terrible wicked person." (Anger, Rage, Fury)

RATIONAL PREFERENCES *(Cont'd)*	IRRATIONAL DEMANDS *(Cont'd)*
9. "It is preferable that I not intentionally or unintentionally make errors in judgment against myself; to do so is regretfully against my best interest." (Sadness, Regret)	"I don't have a right to be wrong, and so therefore I should not make mistakes; when I do falter, I rate as the rotten person that I secretly knew I was all along." (Guilt, Depression)
10. "Granted, being deprived or depriving myself is no picnic, and I naturally possess a strong preference for not going without - I want what I want, when I want it." (Frustration)	"I have to have my piece of taffy at the drop of a hat, and woe is me when I'm required to go without. It's the pits when I can't have my cake and eat it too - plus lose weight besides." (Self-Pity, Listlessness, Inertia)
11. "I usually want and am happier when I get what I think I deserve by way of fairness and justice, and it is damned annoying when I don't strike it rich in those regards." (Displeasure, Irritation)	"I should be the one person in the cosmos to get what he deserves when it is to my advantage to get what I deserve; in that I'm anointed as special, such fairness and justice is my due - even though others haven't come around to admitting it yet." (Resentment, Self-Pity)
12. "When I reach out to be friendly and to make friends with others, I very strongly have hopes for a return on my extension investment and am saddened by the possibility of such returns not occurring." (Sadness, Regret)	"When I put out the welcome mat to someone who has the potential to be my friend, he better not betray my overtures. If he does, I'll loath and despise him until hell freezes over - if not longer." (Betrayal, Bitterness, Hurt)
13. "I find much value in helping others, and when I come across an opportunity to take action as a Good Samaritan, I very much relish being able to do so." (Concern for Others' Well-Being)	"I have to be insistent in helping those whom I feel sorry for at every turn; not taking every opportunity to do so, or faltering in my chances to affirm this sacred value, leaves me with my own disrespect." (Self-Disgust, Other Pity)

RATIONAL PREFERENCES *(Cont'd)*	IRRATIONAL DEMANDS *(Cont'd)*
14. "I don't like pulling public blunders, especially as it promotes my own disadvantages and others' teasing afterwards." (Apprehension, Concern)	"I hate making errors in front of others and must never do so; I especially can't stand the ridicule and chiding that others might throw my way in the mudslinging that follows." (Shame, Demeaningness)
15. "I don't particularly care for the fact that others have advantages that I don't and that I wish that they didn't. Such resources beyond my abilities seem unfair." (Envy, Wishful Motivation)	"Others should not have any advantages that I don't possess, and it is brutally awful and harshly unacceptable when they do." (Jealousy, Self-Pity, Resentment)

All these examples illustrate that humans have two distinct ideas about each of their life circumstances. Most often they start with a preference, wish, or want. Such desires prompt clearheadedness and motivation. Emotional well roundedness and incentive get lost when rational preferences are blown up into irrational demands. Rationality will help make your world go around; irrationality will get you dizzy. When you find your self-talk reeking and raging with "have to"s, "shoulds," "musts," "got to"s, or "ought to"s, switch gears and get yourself back to your original position of preference.

Just as apples made into applesauce were once separate entities, so too were preferences previously set apart from demands. It is this apartness that permits emotional health; fusing the two plants reaps the seeds of emotional upset. Sorting out wants from requirements allows you to avoid running them together, which in turn will permit you to run your life in a way that will take much pressure off yourself and your relationships with others. Repeatedly run your preferences by yourself, as they will spark anticipation and participation and will contribute to your long-range happiness and survival. But don't blend them into commands, as they will run over and ruin your best intentions by allowing them to stray into demands.

Is the Grass Really Greener
On the Other Side?
Hope as Virtue,
False Hope as Vice

A large group of people were observed walking around a tree, called The Tree of Sorrows. One by one they were told that they would be given a once-in-a-lifetime chance to get rid of all their burdens and sorrows forever by simply placing them on the tree branches. Such a deal! The one fly in the ointment was that such a trade-off could only be made under the condition that each person would be required to exchange his or her problems for someone else's. With very little hesitation, every person decided to keep their own difficulties All walked away from this seeming golden opportunity much wiser; all learned the valuable lesson that the grass is not always greener on the other side.

People often discover that the closer they get to achieving a goal, the more tarnished it becomes. This is so because we live in an imperfect world populated by imperfect people. Whether it be an often sought-after relationship, a long-awaited job promotion, spirited anticipation about a move to another part of the country, or a high sense of optimism about observing the emotional growth and development of a child, reality often kills the dream. Yet, humans often hope against hope that the ideals of the dream can be kept alive. There seems to be a catch to practically everything. The problem is that it often can't be seen until you get close up.

Dreams are the mechanism of hopes. This is good and bad. Hopes are best set apart from false hopes, lest the dream become a nightmare. This guide will try to distinguish between the advantages of hopes and the disadvantages of false hopes and will explore the virtues of the first and the vices of the second. Hope in itself is the substance out of which much motivation is made. Without hope, there would be little zest for living. Ambition would get lost in the complacency shuffle. Hope promotes a keener, more decisive state of mind, a sense of alertness, and a feeling of anticipation for and participation in life. However, hopes will eventually be dashed and dreams shattered if they are built upon the sand of wishful thinking rather than the rock of rational thought.

Rational hopes can be set apart from irrational false hopes with the following distinctions:

1. *Occupied with dreams versus preoccupied with daydreams.* Regularly concentrating on your dreams and schemes is one thing; consuming yourself with them is another. Realistic balance of thought allows more of an opportunity to contrast dream possibilities with pipe dream impossibilities.

2. *Thinking makes it so versus doing gets it done.* Dwelling on a possibility long enough is likely to turn it into a probability if not an inevitability in your mind. Extended "thinking" decisions oftentimes are allowed to become an end in themselves and can be made to serve as a convenient substitute for "doing" decisions. When thinking is used as an end in itself, turning dreams into realities will be a never-ending battle.

3. *Illumination versus discoloration.* Hopes bring into clearer focus what color the grass really is on the other side of the fence; false hopes, with their overdone expectations, distort and discolor these other possibilities.

4. *Energizing versus exhausting.* Hopes promote pep and vigor; false hopes, with their impossible dreams and frustrating blind alleys, will poop you out.

5. *Explain versus deny.* Hopes explain life as you would like it to be. They account for your wishes and wants. False hopes deny possible negative realities. They discount any problem possibilities associated with the end result. They fail to consider the tarnish behind the glitter and the gold and that it may be even harder to overcome the problems of being rich than the difficulties of being poor.

6. *High frustration tolerance (HFT) versus low frustration tolerance (LFT).* Hopes are established with an acceptance of the realistic amount of effort that will likely be required to achieve a given result. False hopes are often set up by overlooking the energy necessary to accomplish desired ends. Low frustration tolerance tendencies are disguised by focusing on the excitement of possible accomplishment; the exaggerated difficulty of the hunt goes unacknowledged.

7. *Fact versus fantasy.* Hopes are formed in the facts of life as you anticipate them to be. Pseudo-hopes are grounded in fantasy thinking. Such a make-believe view stokes the fires of distorted imagery.

8. *Suggestion versus suggestibility.* Hopes come from an enlightened consideration of your own suggestions. False hopes stem from a blind consideration of others' suggestions.

9. *Missing information versus misinformation.* Hopes develop from dimensions to self that are lacking that you hope to fill. False hopes relate to misinformation about what to unrealistically expect of yourself.

10. *Seeking pleasure versus running from pain.* Pathways of hope are made for offensively wanting something better. Road maps and rainbows of false hopes are created to defensively avoid something worse, to avoid the part of the glass that is empty rather than seek the part that is full.

11. *Fueled by deliberation versus desperation.* Hopes run on wants, false hopes are propelled by alleged needs. The first produces action, concern, and involvement; the second overreaction, consumption, and entanglement.

12. *Seeking success versus avoiding failure.* Hope is often geared toward making what is good, better. False hope is frequently meant to prevent what is bad from becoming worse.

13. *Perspiration versus inspiration.* The effort required to get to the present is likely to motivate the hopeful-acting person to go further. False hope tendencies often wait on a magical, spiritual awaking prior to getting their momentum in gear.

14. *Self-acceptance versus self-proving.* Hopeful people are able to accept themselves whether or not they achieve their hopes. People who act on false hopes secretly believe they are worthless and try to perfume their self-downing by living a fairy tale fantasy life that pictures and proves themselves more to their own liking.

15. *Exciting versus dramatic.* Hopefully searching for and changing your life into something better can make for exciting times. Inventing bigger-than-life illusions multiplies into false ecstasy that is easily attached to and can begin to take on a life of its own, to the neglect of creating the actual experience that you hope for.

16. *Science versus magic.* Hopeful possibilities are based on a decent respect for human limitations and on evidence that what is sought after is obtainable. False hopes reflect an unrealistic "sky is the limit" mentality that often results in a huge emotional letdown when you eventually discover that wishing for the moon does not magically get you there.

17. *Competition versus complacency.* Hopeful-acting people are likely to be in competition with themselves as they try to extend their capacity to get more from life. False hopes, in all their artificial splendor, make it convenient

to lull oneself into thinking that all that is desired can be achieved in a twinkling of an eye.

18. *Long-range versus immediate comfort.* Realistic hopes encourage a long-range view of life. They suggest present pain for future gain; that it's better to feel uncomfortable now while striving for what you want than to feel uncomfortable for a long time as a result of avoiding taking more immediate action. False hopes produce a peculiar sense of smugness as a result of the immediate intensity from fantasy hoopla.

19. *An extension versus a diversion from what is.* Hopes have a foundation, resources to build from; false hopes distract from deficiencies in anticipation that by sweeping them under the rug they will go away.

20. *Express self versus impress others.* Hopes are seen as a natural expression of one's values. False hopes are created to impress upon others what remarkable achievements you are capable of. Such impressions have at their base the goal of gaining exceptional notoriety and acclaim that you believe are necessary to have.

21. *Planned versus random effort.* Hope encourages you to prioritize your goals so you can do a lot of one or a few things; false hopes are not so focused, and you end up doing a little bit of a lot of things but not too much of any one thing. Rather than getting a bead on a bull's-eye, a scattered, shotgun approach is used to track your goals.

22. *Facing versus avoiding conflict.* Hope will likely motivate you to go directly into the mouth of the dragon and face the conflicts associated with actualizing your ambitions. False hopes cover up inevitable conflicts that stem from a presumed peaches-and-cream, smoother-than-silk image of success.

23. *Realize versus wonderfulize.* Realizing and accepting the realities in approaching and achieving the dream are a

reflection of hopefulness. "Wonderfulizing" about the road and the destination itself paints an ultra-idealistic picture that is unlikely to be found on this imperfect planet.

24. *Preference versus demand.* Hopeful ambitions resist the tendency to insist upon success. A decided wish is maintained, while the bull-headed demand of false hope is abandoned.

25. *Time lines versus making up for lost time.* Hopeful-acting people have paid some dues. Their time to press toward their goal has come. False-hoped individuals, because they have procrastinated on paying the fiddler, try to make up for lost time - only to find out that they have backed themselves up against odds and it is too much effort, too late, to try to arrive at their destination.

26. *Self-reliance versus other dependence.* Hopes are more likely to stem from self-sufficiency, while false hopes typically depend on someone else to successfully bring home the bacon.

27. *Active participation versus passive effort.* Hopes spark adrenaline; false hopes substitute form for substance and allow dream possibilities to attend to themselves. False hopes make it easy to falsify the effort required to turn a dream into a reality.

Hopes and false hopes can be further distinguished by the belief systems that spawn each. The following contrasting thoughts lead to realistic or unrealistic hopes, depending upon which ones are put into operation at any given point in time:

IDEAS OF HOPE	VERSUS	IDEAS OF FALSE HOPE
"Because my hopes, dreams, and schemes are important, I'd best occupy myself with them so as not to lose sight of their importance."		"Because my hopes are all-important, I have to preoccupy myself with them, even if it means not seeing the forest for the trees in losing perspective to them."

IDEAS OF HOPE *(Cont'd)* VERSUS IDEAS OF FALSE HOPE *(Cont'd)*

"It's best that I not let thinking about my hopes take on a life of its own. It's better that I realize, accept, and take action on the idea that doing *not* thinking gets it done."	"How exciting and fantastic it is to think about my ambitions. That way I can gratify myself about all their glamorous possibilities without even lifting a finger."
"The grass may be greener on the other side; how interesting it may prove to be to try to find out."	"The grass absolutely has to be greener on the other side; I am going to sit here and feast on my grand hopes until I know for sure."
"How energizing it is to be on the cutting edge of new possibilities for my life."	"I can't figure it out. I try and I try some more, wearing my fingers to the bone to achieve my ultimate dreams, and what do I get? - bony fingers."
"True, the reality roadblocks en route to my dreams are going to be difficult. However, it is not true that I have to deny the existence of these obstacles or intimidate myself by them."	"Achieving my hopes is just too much effort. It's so much simpler and just as enjoyable to fantasize about them; after all, dreams are better than realities anyway."
"This is what I truly want to do with my life."	"This is what authorities who know more about what is best for me than I do think I should do with my life. It's best that I follow the suggestions of these eminent people with such infinite wisdom."
"There are gaps in my development that I hope to more fully fill."	"The sky is the limit and I have to fulfill my unlimited potential."
"I am making myself feel and am making my life go okay - but I want to make myself feel and make my life go better."	"I want to make life less painful, to be less miserable, and to see to it that life gets worse at a slower rate."
"I want to achieve my goals and accomplish my ends to the best of my ability."	"I definitely have to achieve my goals and accomplish my ends well beyond the best of my ability."

IDEAS OF HOPE *(Cont'd)* **VERSUS IDEAS OF FALSE HOPE** *(Cont'd)*

"I want to make my life better under my current self-acceptance umbrella."	"I have to succeed to prove to myself and others that I am truly a worthwhile person."
"It's best that I sprightly but deliberately strive for more advantages in my life."	"If I have to frantically knock myself out, if not kill myself, or bust a gut (to prove that I am superhuman), so be it."
"Is there evidence that what I seek after is within my reach and grasp?"	"To hell with any evidence that my goals are obtainable; my fairy godmother will magically make things right."
"To compete with myself in an effort to extend my abilities and advantages is perhaps the most meaningful thing that I could pull off in my lifetime."	"Now that I've got my ducks in order by way of goals, I'll sit back and see what happens from here."
"Granted, I am exchanging short-range pain for long-run gain. However, my present pain is a small price to pay for my lengthier gain. I accept that it's not easy to take the easy way out and that the line of least resistance is often the line of most resistance."	"I just cannot stand to wait for long-run comfort. By letting my dreams take on a life of their own, I don't have to wait because I can feed off my fantasies rather than painfully create my realities."
"What better way to express myself than to actively confirm and affirm my values."	"By blowing up my hopes and dreams, I can impress others and get them to like me and approve of me more."
"Better that I concentrate on one or a few things at a time so I don't end up doing a little bit of a lot of things but not too much of any one thing."	"The more the merrier. If I flood myself with goals, I am sooner or later going to touch on achieving at least one of them."
"I want to build upon my resources."	"I have nothing to fall back on, and with my many fleeting schemes I can put that fact out of my mind, at least for the moment."

IDEAS OF HOPE *(Cont'd)*   **VERSUS   IDEAS OF FALSE HOPE** *(Cont'd)*

"Conflict is a fact of life. I can accept this as part of the territory of goal seeking."

"Conflict has more discomfort than I can bear. Living my hopes in my head lets me avoid such utter unpleasantry."

"I've paid my dues. What I want is not a fly-by-night goal. I'm ready to actively participate in seeking and, if necessary, stalking what I want."

"I've dragged my feet for so long that it will take too much time and effort to make up for lost time; let me dream on."

Hope is a life's blood and will give you an added lease on life. False hope leaches blood, draining and dampening future possibilities. To gain more virtue and less vice by way of hope, equip yourself with the following suggestions:

1. *Know what to realistically expect from self, others, and life.* Happiness is a direct ratio between what you expect and what you get. In defining your hopes, take on moderate expectations.
2. *Distinguish rational thinking from rationalizing.* Rationally explain to yourself the realities behind the dream that are not going to go away. Do this instead of burying your head in the sand, assuming that if you explain them away, they will go away.
3. *Don't wait for the spirit to give you utterance.* See that inspiration comes from perspiration and that the best way to learn what your capabilities might be is to get behind yourself and push. Such a philosophy of sustained effort had best be put forth whether you are in the mood to do so or not.
4. *Don't wonderfulize.* Develop a healthy sense of skepticism to balance the human tendency to look at the world through rose-colored glasses.

5. *Don't awfulize.* Whether you dramatize the good or the bad, wonderfulize or awfulize, you are likely to get the same avoidance result, albeit for different reasons. If you think something is going to turn out simply wonderful, there is no reason to attend to it. If something is predetermined to turn out "awful," it will likely be avoided due to the surplus pain associated with it.

6. *Don't necessitize.* See that your life doesn't depend on realizing your ambitions. If you make your dreams your lifeline, you are likely to distort their significance for your future. Fulfilling dreams is nice but not necessary.

7. *Unconditionally accept yourself.* If you can accept yourself regardless of the outcome of your hopes, you will be more likely to keep them in perspective and seek them more clearheadedly.

8. *Examine your premises.* Above all, look at your belief systems that are the cornerstones of your hopes. What you hope for is not as important as the reasons you seek what you want.

Have and hold hopes and dreams for your life. Hang on to the idea that the grass *could* be greener on the other side. Try to be happier with your lot in life while hopefully striving for something better. However, keep in mind that just as the road to hell is paved with good intentions, the path toward heavenly ideals might be sugarcoated with glittering, false ideas. Abandon pipe dreams that assume an automatic pot of gold at the end of the rainbow. Understand that no one has "promised you a rose garden." Yet, try to hopefully, rather than woefully, plant your own garden while trying to make the grass around it as green, if not greener, than that on the other side. By virtue of your efforts you can gather factual information and avoid the vice of expecting too much or too little.

Note. From *Feeling Right When Things Go Wrong* by Bill Borcherdt. Copyright © 1998, Professional Resource Exchange, Inc., P.O. Box 15560, Sarasota, FL 34277-1560.

Thirteen Scripts That People Invent: Uninvention as a Means of Discovering Emotional Well-Being

"Where did I ever get that idea?" The assumption behind this common question is that the notion being considered was obtained if not imposed from without, for instance, by parents, culture, or teachers. Beliefs are not rubber-stamped on their holders. Ideas that humans use to run their lives are not molded into their psyche. Rather, humans make up ideas in their head. Such concoctions, though often fictional, are self-manufactured. This is the bad news. The good news is that any idea that is believed can be disbelieved. There are advantages to understanding that humans aren't scripted so much as they script themselves. These include:

1. *Affirms free will.* Comfort can be gained from knowing that an ever-reachable human freedom is the ability to think whatever one chooses to think about any circumstance.
2. *Creates a self-inspired values realization platform.* Knowing that you were an active participant rather than a passive recipient in determining your values allows you to more easily spring toward updated views that have potential for creating increased clearheadedness.

3. *Opposes fatalistic, deterministic notions that convenience do-nothingism.* After all, if you had had reference points for guiding your life implanted in you by others, how could you possibly dislodge such ideas, however faulty and self-defeating they might be?

4. *Minimizes other blame.* Discouraging yourself from foolishly blaming others for what you thought was their poisoning of your mind has its emotional self-sufficiency advantages.

5. *Heads off the sulking, whining, moaning, and groaning that is seen under the umbrella of self-pity.* There is less likelihood of feeling sorry for yourself when you acknowledge responsibility for your value system.

6. *Encourages looseness and informality in your associations.* A self-choosing model takes away any fears that come from what you think others have done or might do to you. This allows a more freewheeling relationship with your social group.

7. *Promotes a more experimenting lifestyle.* A larger sample of the good things in life is likely to be gained by realizing that you can guide your own mind with your own ideas in testing the waters of opportunity. Knowing that you can give yourself the green light rather than wait for an authority's permission to do so filters into a renewed sense of involvement in life.

8. *Makes possible an increased influence on others.* In a social situation the person who is able to think more flexibly is likely to have the most influence. Knowing that you determine your own thought permits you to not waste time in second-guessing yourself about what others might advise. More direct, stronger persuasion is likely to occur when leading with your own script rather than secondhandedly following someone else's notion.

9. *More concentrated effort.* Focusing on a self- rather than other-choosing stance provides you with the capacity to focus on doing a lot of one thing that you find important rather than a little bit of a lot of things that others might want to steer you toward.

10. *A philosophy of admittance with its advantages thereof is founded.* Best of all, and woven through all the preceding advantages, is that admitting to your own self-indoctrination puts you more in the saddle seat of your life. Confidence in your ability to de-indoctrinate yourself from faulty notions toward those in your long-range best interest is increased when you admit to your talent to deceive yourself by your own, and not someone else's, transposed values platform.

Our social and family systems teach standards and preferences. Individuals tend to inflate these recommended guidelines into absolutes and demands. Having standards and preferences to be sought after in a flexible, well-thought-out way is what helps make the world go around. Amplifying such desires into rigid insistencies will make you dizzy. Following societal suggestions to want a good love and sex life, parental instruction to desire a good job, and teachers' encouragements to value good grades will encourage a well-thought-out sense of involvement. Dictating to yourself that, because such accomplishments would be to your advantage, you are mandated by universal law to achieve them will bind you up emotionally and disrupt your efforts. Spelling out preferences is culture's way of affirming its values. Demanding that these preferences be gained is the perfectionistic component of human nature that had best be loosened. Such all-or-nothing thinking will bring emotional havoc.

Following are some examples of self-developed frozen judgments that, left unchecked, will poison personal happiness. Each is a self-styled misery proclamation that represents human tendencies toward personalization, overgeneralization, exaggeration, overreaction, demandingness, or downingness. Each script of invention has the net effect of an invisible emotional straitjacket; its description is followed by (a) faulty unprovable ideas (FUI) that reflect its position, (b) negative outcomes (NO), and (c) countering rational ideas (CRI) that make convenient (d) more favorable outcomes (MFO) of an unbinding, unwinding, as opposed to unbending, nature.

1. *"If I fail, I'm a failure."* This overextended view of self judges the whole by one part of it. A person who fails at a given project is just someone who came up short in performance, not someone who is complete with failure. To be correct, such an overgeneralized position would be required to prove not only that the person failed in the present but has always failed in the past and will always fail in the future. An unlikely reality! The myth that if you lose at something you're a loser is seen in the following faulty ideas. Left unquestioned, they will block a more hopeful view of your potential for happiness.

   (FUI):

   • "Not only do I do my behavior, but I am my behavior."
   • "What I do is the same as who I am."
   • "The act represents the actor."
   • "One part is equal to the whole."
   • "Because one part is bad, the rest is bad also."
   • "People who do bad things are bad people."
   • "When I do something stupid, I'm stupid."
   • "If I don't condemn myself for my poor performances, I'll never correct them."
   • "I deserve to look down on myself when I act poorly."
   • "Labeling myself as a total failure will motivate me to do better in the future."
   • "If I try I might fail. If I fail I'd be a schmuck. So I'll avoid failure and schmuckhood by not trying."

(NO):

a. *The self-fulfilling promise.* Believing that you're an absolute failure does not lend itself to the possibility of succeeding in the future. This single-minded idea affirms your failure identity and confirms your future failings.

b. *Conveniently, "accidentally on purpose," excuses future efforts.* "After all, because I'm such a complete failure, I can save myself some energy and continue to lie down to rest, not even bothering to try to change what has always existed and will always continue to exist."

c. *Promotes a sheltered life.* Believing that failure is shattering to your very being will discourage taking a more experimenting, adventuresome approach to life.

d. *Encourages self-downing.* To qualify as a failure, one would by definition be a failure through and through. Such a self-imposed totality often paves the way toward giving yourself a report card with a bad mark.

e. *Invites a "Birds of a feather flock together" outlook.* People who identify themselves as failures tend to seek out the companionship of others who have a similar view of themselves. These associations will likely feed on themselves and encourage even more self-defeating attitudes and behaviors.

(CRI):

- "When I fail, I qualify as a person who failed and not as a failure."
- "Correction yes! Condemnation no!"
- "Stupid behavior by a nonstupid person."
- "I don't avoid failure by not trying; I guarantee it. However, whether I fail by trying and not succeeding or by not trying, I cannot prove that I am, nor will I rate myself as, a failure."

- "Failing is bad, but I'm not bad."
- "Compassion had best begin at home. I refuse to put myself down for my failures."
- "It's best that I associate more with those who are pretty good at what I eventually would like to succeed in."
- "I do my behavior but I'm not my behavior."
- "I, like all other humans, am too complex and ever-changing to be rated by the things I accomplish or fail to accomplish."
- "Perhaps if I didn't place everlasting judgments on myself, I would give myself more opportunity to test out what I have the potential to be successful at."
- "I may fail at what I want to accomplish, but I will never fail as a human being."
- "People who lose are not losers."

(MFO):

a. *An expanded life.*   When failure is understood to not be shattering, a larger sampling of what is available in life will likely be experienced.   A cocoon existence can be transformed into a butterfly life.

b. *The more tastes, the tastier the experience.*   The more you search and research new opportunities, the more advantages you will likely find.   If you experiment much, you will sometimes succeed and sometimes fail.   If you experiment little, you will seldom succeed.

c. *Feelings of well-being that stem from unconditional self-acceptance.*   Perhaps the most efficient way to take pressure off yourself is to accept yourself regardless of performance outcome.

d. *More social advantages.*   As you cut yourself some emotional slack, your associates are likely to find you more fun to be around.   Freeing yourself up from overconcerns about failure permits you to approach your social contacts in a more easygoing manner.

e. *Conveniences success.* As you focus less on the alleged horrors of failure, you can better concentrate on putting into practice a plan for success.

2. *"Others' opinion = me."* This other-dependent self-statement places you at the mercy of another's opinion. Believing that others' review of you represents you results in you being beholden to them. If this equation were accurate, feelings of emotional well-being would rely on others' favoritism. Counterconcluding that others' viewpoints about you reflect what is likable for them rather than being a personal reflection on you provides the substance out of which self-acceptance is made. Unless debated, this faulty notion will create emotional intimidation about the possibility of disapproval. Fear and anger are likely to be produced from this emotionally dependent state: fear of losing the seemingly required positive acknowledgment, and anger at the other for abandoning you in your dire need for approval. Because dependent, fearful, and angry people don't blend very well with their social group, the end result is likely to be relationship disruption rather than lubrication.

(FIJI):

• "I need other people's approval and I have to persist until I get it."
• "What others think of me is much more important than what I think of myself."
• "How I feel about myself is directly related to how others view me."
• "I'm nobody until somebody else thinks I'm somebody."

- "Others' reviews of me are sacred, so I have to find my salvation in others' favoritisms."
- "Others thinking poorly of me makes me feel inferior, so I have to perfume my downhood by getting others to think well of me."
- "I can't stand it when others think less of me."
- "Because others' approval is the key to my happiness, I must control for it by controlling them in getting them to like me."

(NO):

a. *Emotional exhaustion.*   Energy is evaporated from trying to save yourself from what you believe to be the never-ending wrath of others' disapproval.

b. *Fear, panic, desperation.*   Overconcerning yourself about the possibility of losing yourself in the event of another's dislike is likely to produce an anxiety-ridden state of mind.

c. *Blocks personality well-roundedness.*   Basing decisions more on what others think rather than what you think at best restricts your experiences and self-discoveries.   Letting others call your decision-making shots shoots down a broader exposure to life.

d. *Drives people away.*   People who create dire needs for approval are not very enjoyable to be around.   Respect for and comfort in another's presence are lost as a result of the approval-seeker's urgent pleas for eternal approval.

e. *Results in trying to prove yourself to the neglect of being yourself.*   Efforts to convince others to have a high opinion of you are emphasized to the neglect of acting like yourself.   Psychological cosmetics end up disguising your truer colors.   Consequently, a more zestful approach to living is extinguished.

(CRI):

- "I can be myself without thinking I have to prove myself."
- "Others' opinions represent their tastes, likes, and dislikes and have nothing to do with my value to myself."
- "I can be an enjoying person in my own right - apart from what others think of me."
- "Best I not necessitize; others' affirmative judgments are nice, but hardly necessary."
- "Granted, disapproval is not the greatest thing in the world and is certainly nothing to do cartwheels about. However, others' negative judgments are tolerable and certainly not bigger than life or beyond reality."
- "Will the world stop spinning on its axis, the sun burn out, or the moon turn to green cheese if someone doesn't like me or threatens not to like me? I doubt it!"

(MFO):

a. *More social attractiveness.*   The less guarded and defensive you are about others' opinion of you, the more favorably disposed they are likely to be toward you.
b. *Increased task efficiency.*   The less worrisome you make yourself about others' critiques of your performances, the better able you will be to concentrate on and fine-tune your performance.
c. *Increased vim, vigor, and vitality.* Energy saved from brooding about what others might be thinking about you can be reinvested in pursuing projects and pleasures that are enjoyable for you.
d. *Increased participation in life.* Knowing that you wouldn't be required to put yourself down in the

event of disapproval conveniences a more eventful life.

3. *"Because something is good, I have to have, do, or need it."* Humans naturally have preferences and standards; these are also reflected to them via their society's values. For instance, society may say that it's preferable or better to earn a fair amount of money, to be thin, to have a good love life, to be well liked. But then individuals elevate these values into the bottomless pit of demands, that is, "Because something is good, it's required." This perfectionistic insistence that standards be followed to a tee plants a lot of emotional wear and tear that reaps harvests of anxiety, anger, and self- or other-downing. Seeking the ambitions that one finds desirable makes the world go around, because such strivings pump meaning into life. It is the demand that you have to have or need your preferences that puts pressure on you and causes disillusionment.

(FUI):

- "I need what I want."
- "I can have - and need it all."
- "Deprivation is awful; I must not be deprived and I can't stand it when I am."
- "My advantages make me a better person, so to qualify for angelhood I have to have all the advantages that the world has to offer."
- "I deserve the best, so when opportunities to gain such offerings exist, being the deserving person I am, I have to go after possessing them in a possessed way."
- "If I don't put undue pressure on myself to get what I want, I'll likely never get it."

- "If I don't demand that I gain what I find worthy of having, I'm likely to go to the other extreme and turn myself into a lifeless, unmotivated person."

(NO):

a. *A hard-pressed existence.* All work and no play makes Jack a dull boy. Blowing out of proportion how important goal achievement is makes for a similar shallow, blunted existence. It is very taxing to continually shoot for the moon by magnifying desires into demands.

b. *Relentless disappointments.* Putting your wishes and wants on a pedestal will often result in you and them being knocked down. Due to limits of time, energy, and human potential, you are likely to often come up short in attaining your wishes. Because happiness is a direct ratio between what you expect and what you get, being conservative in your wants and then not exalting those same desires into necessities would be advisable.

(CRI):

- "I don't have to have, nor do I need what I want."
- "Why must I be the one person in the universe who is not deprived and always gets what he wants?"
- "Never deprive a person of the right to go without; deprivation can be good for me in that it permits me to appreciate what I have."
- "Although gaining advantages makes me better off, they do not make me a better person. If I don't judge myself by them I can then afford to go after them in a deliberate rather than a desperate, demanding way."
- "Fortunately, there is no deservingness in life in that I wouldn't always want to get what I deserve."

- "There are ways to more wholesomely motivate myself than to place abundant pressure on myself."
- "Because I give up my demandingness and care less doesn't mean that I have to give up and become uncaring."

(MFO):

a. *More peace of mind.* By accepting the gap between what you want and what you get and by convincing yourself that you don't need what you value, you unblock yourself from self-inflicted demandingness while unlocking the door to a more clearheaded state of mind.

b. *Goals are sought for the right reasons.* Continue to seek out your goals but with the added advantage of doing so for the right, preferential reasons rather than for the wrong, demanding reasons.

c. *Minimizes overfocusing on and pitying of self.* Instead of feeling sorry for yourself like the baby who didn't get his milk, such self-indulgences can be avoided by a more enlightened view of going without.

d. *Depressure without demotivation.* Incentive does not have to be an endurance test. Motivation by preference rather than demand will likely lead to more efficient and enjoyable goal seeking.

4. *"If something is bad or painful, it must not happen to me."* This childish insistence that disadvantages or discomfort be endlessly avoided is related to the babe-in-the-cradle notion that the world was made for you. This infantile assumption implies a low tolerance for frustration. It can be combated by an understanding that you are not in the world to feel comfortable, but to experience the world - which will likely include a fair amount of discomfort. Failure to acclimate yourself to inevitable

negative happenings will result in a continued low threshold for emotional discomfort and avoidance patterns.

(FUI):

- "I can't stand discomfort and so I have to avoid it at all costs."
- "The world and people in it should see to it that I experience nothing but the comforts of home."
- "The universe runs in orderly cycles rather than randomly, and it should be ordered to promote me nothing but pleasures and not some things like pain."
- "Comfort is sacred, pain is evil. Nothing but good can come from comfort; nothing but bad can come from pain."
- "After I pay my growing-pain dues, nothing but pleasant things should be due me."

(NO):

a. *Limited life exposure.* Insisting on pleasure excuses abandoning a broader range of experiences that can only be accomplished by risking pain.

b. *Conveniences a philosophy of whiningness.* Screaming for only the good things in life is the result of and reinforces a pampered view of self.

c. *Leads to anger and vindictiveness.* When your pleas for a womblike, comforting existence aren't met, resentment toward the people and forces you hold accountable for your sometimes unpleasant existence are likely to be brought into play.

d. *Greater likelihood of giving up.* Ongoing expression of a low emotional threshold will encourage throwing in the towel in the face of what you have concluded is a never-ending pains-taking world.

(CRI):

- "What does the world and people in it really owe me by way of comfort - or anything else for that matter? A big fat nothing, that's what!"
- "I live in a haphazard, random universe. As a consequence of this grim but not too grim reality, I am more than likely to experience a share, unfair or fair, of pain as well as pleasure."
- "Comfort is nice but not necessary."
- "I can tolerate, stand, or bear anything - as long as I am alive. If this would ever cease to be the case I would die - and hopefully my benefactors would be nice enough to give me a decent burial."
- "The dues I have paid for my growing pains makes me a dues-paying, card-carrying member of the human race - but it does not qualify me for any other special advantages such as guaranteed, unending pleasures or comforts."
- "Apparently I am not special or anointed to be the one person in the whole universe to experience chronic pleasure."

(MFO):

a. *Peace accompanying acceptance.* Resigning yourself to the prospect of pain brings the relief that reflects your less guarded, more tolerant outlook.
b. *Increased persistence.* Perseverance against odds means you are likely to try longer and harder after you acclimate yourself to the pain required to go through to achieve a given result.
c. *Freer choices toward healthier emotions.* Bringing an end to challenging the random laws of the universe puts the brakes on emotional anguish and the accelerator moving toward more in your best interest feelings

of hope, happiness if not joy, and excitement if not exhilaration.

d. *More impact on those around you.* Cutting back on the drama you use to describe your distaste for life's sometimes smelly conditions is likely to result in others hearing and considering more the content of your concerns.

5. *"If something bad has happened, especially repeatedly, it will likely as not have to continue to happen."* This fatalistic position douses the flames of hope for the future. Because you have failed at a given project (up until now) does not mean that you have to continue to do so. History does not have to assume to be or be made to repeat itself. To think that it does is a barrier to potentially bigger and better things. Such a philosophy of unquestioned business as usual contains the seeds of its own destruction before even getting out of the starting blocks.

(FUI):

• "What goes around will continue to go around - no matter what."
• "History will always repeat itself."
• "Once you learn how to do something wrong, you can't unlearn it."
• "Old habits will always stick with you."
• "Whatever will be will be, and what will always be is what has always been."
• "An old dog can't learn new tricks."
• "There's nothing new under the sun."

(NO):

a. *An evacuation of wants.* Why bother to aim for something better if nothing but more of the same can be gained? This desireless state of being contrasts with a more alert, hopeful, bolder view of future possibilities.

b. *Boredom and depression.* Not seeking additional stimulation in life will deteriorate into sitting down and dying a slow emotional death due to your deterministic assumptions.

c. *Social isolation.* Your social group is less likely to gravitate toward you due to your dead-end view of life.

(CRI):

- "Yesterday, today, and forever need not be one and the same, if I can help it - and I can."
- "The whole world is changing; why do people (like myself) have to stay the same?"
- "Doing rather than stewing is the better of the two."
- "Because I've failed, it doesn't mean I have to continue to fail."
- "Thomas Edison tried to invent the light bulb over six hundred times before succeeding. Isn't it a good thing that he didn't think he was going to repeat his failures forever?"
- "There are plenty of old dogs who have learned new tricks."
- "Repetition is the mother of learning *and un*learning."

(MFO):

a. *Increased aspirations, hopes.* Understanding that the future can be different from the past can launch a healthier sense of anticipation.

b. *A disruption of emotional roadblocks.* Lethargy, listlessness, and hopelessness are replaced by hopefulness, alertness, and activity.

c. *Increased quality of social contacts.* Your rekindled sense of vitality will likely attract a more wholesome support system.

6. *"If something to my advantage never happened in the past, it could not occur in the future."* This idea implies that if you have never experienced a favorable love relationship, harmony with your vocation, mastered a musical instrument, or been able to complete some other desired accomplishment, such possibilities will remain forever beyond your reach. New frontiers and possibilities are disallowed with this outlook, which amounts to simply marking time.

(FUI):

- "Before I attempt something that I have not been able to make happen in the past, I need a guarantee that my efforts will pay off."
- "It's too hard to work with a no-cut contract, especially knowing that I have been disqualified in the past."
- "What's the use?"
- "You can't have everything; I'll just be satisfied with the few crumbs I have rather than go for a larger piece of the loaf."
- "I'm going to wait for it to happen rather than try again to make it happen."
- "Good things are guaranteed for those who are patient, I'll just put things in neutral until my ship comes in."

(NO):

a. *Stagnation and sameness.* No movement in a given direction leaves a continued vacuum of accomplishment. A faceless existence and its accompanying emotional numbness are created.

b. *Excuses not trying.* Bad habits of procrastination are practiced in putting off until tomorrow what you haven't been successful at up until today.

c. *Restriction of ambitions.* Evacuating wants via this fatalistic method hampers meaning gained from vital absorption in until-now-unsuccessful projects.

(CRI):

- "If I wait for my ship to come in, I'll probably be at the airport when it finally does."
- "Nothing (ad)ventured, nothing gained."
- "If I can predict tomorrow's results so accurately, why don't I just invest in the stock market and get rich quick?"
- "My present advantages weren't gained overnight or handed to me on a silver platter. I'd better accept that nothing works but working, doing gets it done, and begin anew to renew my efforts to create for tomorrow that which I have not been able to create up until today."
- "Why shouldn't I have to go down a few or even a good number of blind alleys before I find my way home?"

(MFO):

a. *Increased likelihood of success.* Learnings through trial-and-error failings can be put to good use in producing future successes.

b. *Increased frustration tolerance.* Present struggles to create the seeming improbable in the present heighten your ability to better deal with the inevitable dissatisfactions of getting what you don't want or not getting what you do want in the future.

c. *Increased enthusiasm for living.*   Knowing that you have the potential to do what you have not yet done pumps up your perspiration from which inspiration can then flow.

7. *"I have to follow my upbringing; if a significant other once said it, it must be true."*   This unquestioning outlook results in failure to reexamine original ideas you heard from those in authority. P. T. Barnum underestimated when he said there is a sucker born every minute. This tendency toward gullibility had best be disputed with such scientific questioning as "Where is the evidence that (a) I have to follow my upbringing or (b) any particular opinion is founded in fact?" Left unattended, this notion will lead to leading your life by family superstitions.

(FUI):

- "I should not question authority. If I do it means I'm disrespectful and ungrateful toward those I should be looking up to."
- "It's easier to let someone do my thinking for me - it's too hard to think for myself."
- "Others know more about what is best for me to believe than I do."
- "If I follow others' recommendations instead of my own, I can blame them when things go wrong."
- "I need the acceptance and approval of all significant people in my life. If I take issue with their values they might withhold their love and approval, and that would be too much to bear."
- "Opposing traditional values feels too awkward to change; it's not worth the discomfort."
- "Those from whom I might differ might scorn, ridicule, demean, or discredit me for my free thinking, so to avoid becoming less of a person in their eyes, I'll go along with the gag."

(NO):

a. *Excessive worry.*   Making yourself dependent on external authority encourages worrying about escaping its wrath at disobedience.

b. *Mistakes repeated.*   Unthinkingly following someone else's nose and what they think is best for them rather than following your own and what you think is best for you duplicates mistakes that come from such a wrong fit.

c. *Loss of refreshing individuality.*   Having your mind made up to copy others' suggestions rather than create your own leaves you without distinctive values you can call your own.

d. *Lost opportunities.*   Hanging your hat mainly on others' suggestions prevents you from testing out your potential as reflected in your own ideas.

(CRI):

- "I can better learn from the consequences of my own decisions than by letting somebody decide for me."
- "One person, making his or her own decisions, constitutes a majority of one."
- "Any criticisms I receive for making up my own mind represent others' tastes and values, not mine."
- "If I stay with the discomfort that I associate with change, eventually I'll acclimate myself to it rather than startle myself by it."
- "I'm not a trained seal, rat, or guinea pig; I can condition myself toward believing what I deem to be in my best interest."
- "What is considered normal by way of public opinion often is not healthy."

(MFO):

a. *A database that is befitting for you.* Making your own choices leaves you with learnings that piggy-backed off your ideas and not someone else's.

b. *Freewheelingness.* Use of your own mind rather than mindlessly following others frees you up to go in whatever direction you believe best.

c. *The comforts of self-reliance.* Knowing you don't depend on others to find value in your existence generates advantages of self-acceptance and self-confidence.

8. *"My deficiencies = my worthlessness."* This misery equation will get you down on yourself for your fallible nature. Unless uninvented it will create a low-grade, chronic depression at best. This rating game where you give yourself a report card with a bad mark for your bad traits and features is perhaps the favorite human pastime.

(FUI):

- "When I act badly, I'm bad."
- "People who are efficient at something are better people than those who are deficient at the same thing."
- "To have a fault is something to be ashamed of, bigger than life, and the worst of all possible crimes."
- "People who commit errors are weak, inferior beings. Those who do right are strong and noble."
- "I have to do perfectly well or else I'm perfectly worthless."

(NO):

a. *Defensiveness, refusal to admit it when wrong.* Thinking that doing well is sacred often results in denying wrongdoing.

b. *Ongoing disadvantages.* As a result of not admitting mistakes, you are likely to continue to suffer from their negative consequences.

c. *Continued fear and insecurity.* Fear of defaulting, along with its presumed diminishment of self, puts you on thin ice in promoting emotional comfort.

d. *A camouflaged sense of self.* Making your deficiencies the most well-kept secret you have is not the best way to promote your mental health. Transparency and revealingness without shame would be a better way of establishing a more visible, solid sense of being.

(CRI):

- "If my car had a flat tire it wouldn't mean my car is no good. If I give a flat performance it doesn't mean I'm no good."
- "People who admit their mistakes are emotionally strong and secure enough to be able to do so."
- "Being human means to not try to be perfect."
- "I don't have to shame myself about anything."
- "Lighten up without giving up."
- "My deficiencies represent something *about* me; they don't identify me. I'm too complex to rate."

(MFO):

a. *More frequent risk taking.* Knowing that you don't have to put yourself down for anything conveniences a more spirited approach to life.

b. *Less dependence on success to create your happiness.* Knowing that if one part of your life is flawed your whole existence doesn't have to be blown to smithereens allows you to appreciate more what you have than brood about what you don't have.

c. *Self-confidence rather than efficiency or success confidence.* Realizing that you don't have to blame or damn yourself for your undesirable traits and features puts your confidence level above the external prop of success.

d. *Allows people to more fully know you and to gravitate more toward you.* As you expose your blunders, others may see the human side of you, making it easier for them to be more favorably disposed toward you. Humans prefer to associate with humans, not superhumans.

9. *"Others' deficiencies = their worthlessness."* Instead of blaming yourself for your flaws, others are condemned for theirs. Passing judgment on yourself for your deficiencies will get you depressed; rating others with a zero mark will cause anger. This idea gone unchallenged results in a sensitive, prickly approach to self and others.

(FUI):

- "Others are to be blamed and condemned for their faults."
- "Others have to do perfectly well or else they are perfectly worthless."
- "People have to have (many) talents and skills and be good at practically everything they do to have value to themselves."
- "Others are to be encouraged to feel shame and subhuman when confronted with their human imperfections."

(NO):

a. *Others' resentment.* People usually don't appreciate being judged as inferior for their shortcomings.

b. *On the outside of your social group looking in.* Others will likely exclude you from their association due to your condemning ideas.

c. *Contributes to a godlike view of self.* Getting up on your judgmental soapbox contributes to the illusion that you are the noble anointed judge and jury of others.

d. *Stifles self-compassion.* The more you practice evaluating others by their flaws, the more you are likely to trample on yourself for your own.

(CRI):

• "Humans have faults by virtue of their nature; best they not be condemned for having what comes naturally easy."

• "It is unlikely others will do perfectly well, and it cannot be proven that they are perfectly worthless when they don't."

• "Humans have value to themselves by virtue of their existence; they aren't required to have any special talent or skill before that purpose can be served."

• "When I start by trying to shame others for their faults, I end by practicing shaming myself for mine."

(MFO):

a. *Increased goodwill and support from others.* Accepting others with their faults makes it more convenient for them to gravitate more toward you.

b. *Contributes to your own self-acceptance.* The more you accept others in spite of their shortcomings, the better able you will be to accept yourself apart from your own flaws.

c. *Stockpiles tolerance for a rainy day.* The less frustrated you make yourself today about inevitable human failings, the better you will be able to withstand future disappointments in life.

10. *"My values are sacred; thou shalt have no other values before mine."* Perhaps the most destructive self-invented idea is the exalted notion that others don't have free will, but your will. This insistence on others honoring and obeying your one-way view of life has caused more destruction than all the faulty ideas combined. George Bernard Shaw said, "Patriotism is the belief that your country is the best simply because you happened to be born into it." This holier-than-thou idea, holding that those who are different are unworthier than all, promotes anger that has been known to cause nationalism, war, genocide, and civil violence.

(FUI):

- "Those who think differently than I do are nincompoops to be looked down upon."
- "One way! My way! The way!"
- "Everybody is entitled to my opinion."
- "I have discovered the truth and can't figure out why everyone else isn't eager to share it."
- "My will be done!"
- "Love and agreement go hand in hand, and if others really cared about me more they would patronize my values."

(NO):

a. *Increased likelihood of physical violence.* Playing God will likely have you fighting like the devil in your arrogant attempts to control others.
b. *Poor judgment in decision making.* Thinking that you can do no wrong will result in biting off more than

you can chew in attempting projects that may be beyond your capacity to attain.

c. *Blocking of intimacy.*   It may prove difficult to get close to others when you're so hung up on yourself.

d. *Increased stress and possible health problems.*   Anger produces rather than reduces stress. Stomach upset, high blood pressure, and headaches are some of the physical complications from its expression.

(CRI):

- "I'd best not try and make others over."
- "How can he think so differently from me! EASILY, that's how: it's his nature to do so and he has full entitlement to it."
- "One person's cup of tea is another person's poison."
- "I can appreciate others' search for their values without necessarily affirming their ideas."
- "It would be a boring world if everyone thought alike."
- "If I want to influence others, best I first accept them the way they are."

(MFO):

a. *Increased chances of social impact.*   People are likely to be more inclined to consider what you have to say if you don't present it from such a lofty position.

b. *More likelihood of success with your projects.*   Coming off your godlike perch and learning what to more realistically expect of yourself means you will likely accomplish your goals more often.

c. *More social group harmony.*   Increased "likability" and "lovability" are likely to more frequently occur in that others are more likely to be favorably inclined toward you when they sense you don't think you are better than they are.

d. *Improved sense of humor.* Coming off your values throne better affords you the luxury of not taking yourself so seriously. As Ethel Barrymore said, "You grow up after your first laugh - at yourself."

11. *"If it, they, or I are different, it, they, or I are bad."* The human tendency is to startle oneself and think the worst about people and things that are different. It would be better to appreciate unique differences in life than to intimidate oneself about them. Such judgments are normal in that most people make them, but they are not healthy in that they lead to damnation and disturbance.

(FUI):

- "Those (of us) who think alike are better than those (of you) who think differently."
- "It takes too much time to consider individual differences."
- "You can never be too sure about people who are different from you."
- "Anything or anybody is a fly in the ointment; you'd better watch out."

(NO):

a. *Sameness and complacency.* It's easier to get yourself into a rut when you insist on more of the same.
b. *Cutting off your nose to spite your face.* Advantages from new contacts and ideas are lost from avoiding anything or anybody that smacks of being different.
c. *Chronic stress and tension.* Because the world changes and people in it are different, your insistence on sameness of ideas leaves you poorly prepared to cope with countering realities.

(CRI):

- "Nothing ventured, nothing gained."
- "Variety is the spice of life."
- "I can have the advantages of learning more from someone who doesn't confirm my values."
- "Don't judge a book by its cover."
- "Give yourself (them, or it) the benefit of the doubt."
- "Don't throw the baby out with the bath water."

(MFO):

a. *Expanded horizons.* Experimenting with different slices of life gives you a better picture of what is all in it for you.
b. *A more peaceful coexistence with the world and people in it.* Putting yourself on guard against everything and everybody that is different is not the best way to remain in harmony with your environment. Accommodating differences rather than putting yourself in conflict with them is more becoming to your emotional well-being.
c. *Increased alertness and aliveness.* Exposure to new stimulation revives your attention span for daily living.

12. *"I have to know tomorrow's answers today."* Demanding certainty or surety in a world that has none will leave you emotionally bound up. This command leaves you guessing and groping for the future, to the neglect of enjoying the present.

(FUI):

- "I can't wait."
- "Before I decide to go down path A, I have to know that path B wouldn't have more advantages."

- "I can't stand the idea of putting forth effort to succeed without knowing that I might not."
- "After I know the fruits of what my labor will be, then I'll labor - not a moment before."
- "Trying and failing would be awful, so I'll avoid failure by not trying and instead wait until the gold-plated guarantee of success is mine."

(NO):

a. *Hesitation and indecision.* Riding the fence becomes a way of life in this controlling philosophy.
b. *Conveniences self-blame and jealousy.* He or she who hesitates is likely to lose opportunities. Observing more decisive-acting people seize opportunities that you let slip through your ever-hesitant fingers makes more accessible these self- and other-demotions.
c. *Flooding of anxiety.* Insisting that you be able to move ahead in time implies that dreadful events will happen if you are not able to head them off at the pass with such leapfrog efforts. This self-created tear of the unknown quantities that lie ahead is often made to feed upon itself.
d. *Anger and resentment.* This dictatorial attitude eventually produces hostility when the command for certainty is not followed by a universe that is impartial and random.

(CRI):

- "There are no right or wrong answers, only answers based on present evidence."
- "I cannot not decide. If I decide to do nothing I've cast my vote for the status quo."
- "I'm not general manager of the universe yet, so I'd best stop making impossible demands of it."

- "There are no guarantees in life except death and lake flies - I'd best accept that grim, but not too grim, reality."
- "Magic wands and carved-in-granite guarantees have I none."

(MFO):

a. *Production of freedom to test the waters of self-potential.* A noninsisting view provides the flexibility to go forth with choices, the results of which will highlight your capabilities and limitations.
b. *Increased movement.* Making quicker choices exposes you to more of life's dimensions, permitting you to pick and choose learnings from each one.
c. *Increased sense of self-responsibility and trust in self.* Making bold choices breeds a view of self that is compatible with personal accountability and responsible living habits.

13. *"The Irrational Trinity."* The worst is saved for last. The foundation for emotional upset is laid with this tripod of ideas that humans make up in their heads. According to rational emotive behavior therapy's theory of emotional disturbance, these three commandments account for practically all emotional upset. No one tells individuals these three perfectionistic notions: "I have to be perfect"; "Others have to treat me perfectly"; and "Life has to be perfectly easy." Parents, teachers, and social systems put out on the table standards and preferences, such as "It's important to do well"; "It's nice to be treated kindly and pleasantly"; "It's desirable and convenient that life fall into place." Rather than stay with these conventions, the individual is quick to invent absolutes (the "have to"s) such as those mentioned earlier and expanded upon on the following pages.

(FUI):

- "I *have to* do perfectly well or else I'm perfectly worthless. My best isn't good enough. I *have to* do whatever I do better than anyone else and better than the last time I did it - or else I'm no damned good. My best isn't good enough - I *have to* do the best."
- "Others *have to* treat me favorably and gently, with no lapses in kindness and consideration, or else they are no damned good. Especially if I'm nice to them, then they for sure have to patronize me back. If they don't do well by me or otherwise tell me what a great person and a scholar I am (like they *have to*), I'll despise and loathe them until the day that they die - and I hope it's soon."
- "Life has to make it easy for me to accomplish my goals and achieve my ends. When the forces of the universe don't convenience me in this way - especially when I bust butt to do my best - I'll whine, procrastinate, feel sorry for myself, and generally give myself a bad case of listlessness and drop ass. I'll get even with this and other planets for not being accommodating to my projects even if it means cutting off my nose to spite my face."

(NO):

a. *Anxiety, guilt, self-downing (following the first commandment).* This "thou shalt not ever be in error" idea results in unnerving yourself about the possibility of failing beforehand and self-incrimination following inevitable less-than-perfect performances.

b. *Anger, hostility, resentfulness, rage, fury (with the second commandment).* Being for themselves, others will often frustrate and deprive you. Insisting that they are mandated not to do so instills in you these harsh feelings.

c. *Self-pity, lacklusterness, inertia.* And baby makes three (with the third commandment). This 3-year-old philosophy that the world was made for my comforts, and my comforts only, is a form of self-indulgence that is self-defeating for the purpose of creating incentive.

(CRI):

*   "I can try to do well without busting a gut to prove that I am superhuman. I can do the best I can and then go home and forget about it. Because I would like to succeed, it doesn't mean that I have to."
*   "Others can pick and choose, select or not select against me - that is their choice. My choice is whether I'm going to hassle them about their free-willed decision. It will be nice if they patronize my butt, but hardly necessary. (And I don't have to kick them in the butt when they don't.)"
*   "How delightful it is when factors come together in the service of my projects. However, when matters unfairly work out to my disadvantage, I need not pout or pamper myself about going without. I can instead take it with a grin and/or a grain of salt."

(MFO):

a. *Concern, apprehension, self-acceptance.* Hoping to do well and being prepared to acknowledge disappointment when you don't is a healthier way to motivate yourself.
b. *Annoyance, irritation, displeasure.* Expression of dislike when others treat you unkindly is more likely to get their attention while protecting yourself from their future wrath. Furiousness on your part is likely to abandon these constructive purposes.

c. *Vigilance, persistence, determination.* Using your own force in getting behind yourself and pushing will likely gain you more progress than trying to use force on the universe to do your work for you.

Humans are not spoon-fed ideas; they feed themselves. The idea "I was scripted" implies that you were a passive victim of others' teachings rather than an active participant in both your original learnings and in keeping that information alive and influential in your life. Accepting that you fully and foolhardily scripted and continue to script yourself encourages a more active-directive, responsible approach to reducing rather than producing ideas that are to your disadvantage.

Humans are inventors by nature, not nurture. Not only do they invent their technology, they also create their own ideas to explain their world. They come to their worldly explanations with scripts of their own making. Unfortunately, they are talented geniuses at manufacturing distortions that, left unchecked, will leave them indefinitely and near infinitely disturbed. For instance, it is a rare parent who tries to do her child in by trying to teach that he's bad and inferior for getting bad grades on his report card; that he is a loser for losing. What the parent usually intends in her criticisms of the child's performance is to spark a vote of confidence in the child's ability. She is really saying she thinks the child can do better. But because the child has tendencies to overgeneralize and pass judgment on himself to begin with, he is often quick to conclude, "Because my parents are badly criticizing me for my bad report card, I'm bad." It is not the criticism itself that causes the child feeling down, but the unwarranted conclusion that he draws from the facts of the matter.

Just as you, all by your lonesome, diligently produced these unlucky 13 inscriptions, so too can you persist in challenging them. What you originated as a magical invention that led you emotionally astray can be uninvented so as to scientifically discover for yourself more healthful pathways to find your emotional way home. But don't take my word for it. Uninvent and discover for yourself!

Curtailing the "Have to"s Because You Want to: Twenty-Five Good Reasons To Better Dictate Emotional Well-Being by Avoiding Becoming Your Own Worst Dictator

I believe it was George Bernard Shaw who said, "The fact that a true believer is happier than a skeptic is no more to the point than a drunk being happier than a sober person." So, too, rational emotive behavior therapy (REBT) holds that just because you dramatically believe something to be true does not necessarily point to emotional sanity. In fact, REBT holds that emotional disturbance is a frenzied protest against reality, a fanatical refusal to accept what exists; in a word, demanding that what exists not be so. That demand usually comes in the form of a "have to," a "must," a "should," a "got to," an "ought to," or a "supposed to." Emotional disturbance is a preference that has escalated into a demand. When the dictatorial conclusions described above are slackened to a wish, want, desire, or preference, emotional disturbance is better contained. Because word precision is a major factor in promoting emotional well-being, a simple realignment of thought, woven into everyday thinking, can very much increase emotional self-control; demands ("have to"s) moderated into preferences ("would like to"s) can transform emotional disturbance

51

into emotional clearerheadedness. Clients are often pleasantly surprised to learn that after a few days of simply monitoring and minimizing their "have to"s they find themselves more emotionally relieved and less stress-ridden. Consider the following illustrations of demanding, black-or-white, all-or-nothing thoughts that, when countered with more preferentially motivated, well-thought-out ideas, result in encountering a more peaceful state of mind.

DEMANDING SELF-STATEMENTS	NONDEMANDING COUNTERING IDEAS
"I have to do well."	"I would like to do well."
"You have to treat me well."	"I want you to treat me well."
"Life has to come easier."	"I wish advantages more easily would come my way."
"I have to feel more relaxed."	"I wish I were more comfortable."
"I have to know tomorrow's answers today."	"In some ways it would be nice to know the future."
"I have to be loved."	"I want to be loved."
"I have to get what I want."	"I hope to get what I want."
"Life has to be fair and just."	"I wish life were fair and just."
"I have to know for sure."	"I would like to know for sure."
"I have to have approval."	"I prefer to have approval."
"I have to brood about things."	"I tend to brood about things."
"I have to be in control of my emotions."	"I want to be in control of my emotions."
"I have to have understanding."	"I very much want to be understood."
"I have to get agreement."	"I strongly prefer agreement."

DEMANDING SELF-STATEMENTS *(Cont'd)*	NONDEMANDING COUNTERING IDEAS *(Cont'd)*
"I have to be treated the same way that I treat others."	"I would hope to be treated as I treat others."
"I have to win and achieve."	"I'd like to win and achieve."
"I have to follow my upbringing."	"I often tend to want to follow my upbringing."
"I have to believe authority/the authorities."	"I often am inclined to give blind adherence to authority/authorities."
"I have to depend on others."	"I like to depend on others."
"I have to be independent."	"I prefer to be independent."
"I have to take the easy way out."	"I often lean toward taking the easy way out."
"I have to take care of others."	"I like to take care of others."
"I have to be right."	"I'd prefer to be right."
"Others have to take care of me."	"I like it when others take care of me."
"Others have to honor and notice my achievements."	"I hope that others honor and notice my achievements."
"I have to overcome my faults and deficiencies."	"It would be great for me to overcome my faults and deficiencies."
"I have to treat others just like they treat me."	"I tend to treat others just like they treat me."
"Others have to stay out of the way of my goals."	"I like it better when others stay out of the way of my goals."
"I have to be the ideal parent."	"I have hopes for doing well in my parenting role."
"I have to get an erection."	"I want to get an erection."

DEMANDING SELF-STATEMENTS *(Cont'd)*	NONDEMANDING COUNTERING IDEAS *(Cont'd)*
"I have to get an orgasm and it has to be simultaneous with my mate's."	"It would be great for my mate and me to achieve orgasms at the same time, as I desire."

This list is but a sampling of the areas of life into which humans bring their dictates. They practically always come to their life circumstances by defining their goals as good and desirable, but end with the notion that "Because what I want is good, I have to have it." Consequently, they paralyze themselves emotionally, often defeating their original goals. If they would simply hang on to their preferences rather than escalate them into demands, they would be less likely to freeze themselves in their tracks toward goal achievement.

REBT clearly states that nothing in life has to be. To think otherwise is to approach life in a white-knuckled, pressured tone. After reviewing with a client the emotional fallout of the "have to"s, I asked her to tell me in her own words what that discussion meant for her. She replied, "the 'have to's are too definite." Whenever you demandingly tack on a "have to" to your original preference, you plant the seeds of your own emotional destruction. To opt for the containment of emotional disturbance, use scientific thinking backed by the scientific method. Science is tentative, flexible, ever-changing, and does not get itself locked into dogma - that is, the belief that things and people "have to" be a definite way. In science, if you assert something to be true, it is up to you as the believer to prove your hypothesis; it is not the Doubting Thomas's responsibility to disprove your belief. As far as we know, there is no evidence that some things in life are sacred in the sense that they "have to be." The disadvantages of unscientifically buying into this narrow, bigoted thought pattern that reeks with absolute insistence include the following:

1. *Creates anxiety.* Whenever you strongly tell yourself that something by necessity has to be, you will likely cringe in your gut and begin to feel anxious about the possibility that your demand may not become a reality.
2. *Is potentially self- and/or other-downing.* When you and/or others inevitably don't do what you "have to" do, the inclination is to follow with a self and/or other rating, for example, "Because I and/or you didn't do the right thing as I and/or you must or have to, one or both of us is no damn good."
3. *Defies free will.* Freedom of choice is taken away by this narrow perspective. "Have to" means one way and only one to the neglect of open-mindedness.
4. *Squelches the use of reason, logic, and the scientific method.* A more mechanical, rigid view is allowed to dominate from the "have to" mentality. Scientific questioning (e.g., "Where is the evidence for the notion that something or someone has to be different than as is?") is abandoned for grandiose, all-or-nothing beliefs (e.g., "Because I prefer that something or someone be a certain way, it has to"). Rather than relying scientifically on repeated observations, the holder of mechanical thinking depends on single impressions: mainly his or her own.
5. *Blocks alternatives.* Problem solving is frozen in that freer thinking is made to give way to "one way," "the way," or "my way" judgments. Rather than brainstorming alternatives, finalistic thinkers keep themselves stuck in their pigeonholed, one-track views.
6. *Results in an emotional double bind.* Damned-if-you-do-and-damned-if-you-don't outcomes stem from insistent thought. If you think that you must, should, or have to do a certain thing - for instance, go to church or visit grandmother's - and you decide to do it, you will likely make yourself feel resentful for following the dictates of some arbitrary authority. On the other hand, if you don't do the activity you think you should do, you are likely to make yourself feel guilty for not pledging to this arbitrary

command. More flexibility deciding what you truly *want* to do avoids this emotional "should I or shouldn't I" emotional dilemma.

7. *Is an expression of arrogance and self-righteousness.* Establishing a universal standard that others "have to" follow gives vent to an elitist, totalitarian, holier-than-thou philosophy.

8. *Increases stress and tension.* Pressure is fueled by trying to find something that doesn't exist - the absolute truth of the "have to"s.

9. *Prohibits personality well-roundedness.* Demanding methods of thought lock you into one way of relatedness, leaving you with little variance in your approach to life.

10. *De-aspires hope.* It is difficult to be hopeful if there is only "the way" when "the way" isn't working.

11. *Makes projects less enjoying.* Putting undue pressure on yourself to complete a project in only a certain way throws cold water on the enjoyment of it.

12. *Stifles creativity.* Restrictive thinking restricts options while creativity flourishes in a climate of permissiveness.

13. *Blocks unconditional self-acceptance.* Perhaps the most anti-mental-health act is to judge yourself. When you falter in doing what "must" or "should" be done, the tendency is to define yourself by such failure. That is, when you violate the alleged universal standards implied in the "have to"s, the self-put-down will practically always follow.

14. *Disrespects individual differences.* "One size fits all" is the message of the "have to"s, implying that the command fits for all people all of the time, to the neglect of human uniqueness.

15. *Encourages fanaticism and dictatorship.* Frenzy feeds the flames of tyranny with the end result being the creation of golden rules, absolutes that must be adhered to rather than democratically and scientifically questioned. Individuality and consensus are set aside in favor of dogma.

16. *Ignores human variability.* In addition to differing from one another, humans differ within themselves, sometimes from one moment to the next. Mechanical outlooks overlook such variances and by doing so discourage personal development.

17. *Denies human limitations.* Humans do not "have to" do the right thing. The sky is not the limit by way of human potential. By demanding that self or others "ought to" do better than they frequently do, undamning self- and other-acceptance is discouraged. Humans will often act in limited ways regardless of how strongly the true believer protests against such realities. Self- and other-damning can be avoided by taking on a more tolerant outlook.

18. *Tries to disallow the human right to be wrong.* Self- and/or others' betrayal of your favored values is inevitable. Whether unintentional *or* intentional, trespassing is allowed by nature of the quality in the human condition called free will.

19. *Encourages anger and hostility.* When you think that you "have to" have or "need" something from your social group - for instance, cooperation, approval, understanding, or agreement - and those provisions are inevitably withheld, you are likely to conclude, "You're not giving me what I have to have and therefore you are destroying me - you bastard."

20. *Puts pressure on your social group.* Associates find themselves discouraged by the pressure put on them by your demands for provisions; if you act like a porcupine toward them, they will likely flee your presence.

21. *Highlights impatience and "terrible two"ness.* Dictating that things have to be made to favorably happen in your direction *yesterday* is a reflection of the childlike insistence that you "have to" get what you want when you want it rather than more maturely accepting that you get what you get when you get it - and not a moment before!

22. *Makes a problem out of the solution.* "Have to"s reflect and create compellingness, desperation, and noncompromise, all of which multiply problems while overlooking solutions.

23. *Enhances destructive alleged human needs.* A "have to" signals an arbitrary definition for happiness and survival - a supposed "need." Convincing yourself that you don't need what you want, by changing the "have to" to a want, can relieve much stress.

24. *Often leads to symptom stress.* Humans have strong tendencies to upset themselves and to upset themselves about being upset. The same "have to" that caused the original upset is frequently pressed into play after the emotional flurry with the self-sentence, "Now that I didn't get what I have to have, I have to control my emotions about my disappointment on the matter." This is akin to the plaque my children gave me years ago that said "Smile Dammit." To tell yourself you "have to" control your emotions prompts an escalation of them.

25. *Seeks perfectionism.* Perfectionism basically means that somebody or something under all conditions, at all times, has to be a certain way. Perfectionism is more elusive than a fart in a jar; it is what a client of mine terms "trying to find a corner in a silo." I think what George Orwell meant when he said that the essence of being human is to not seek the kingdom of God, and what Vicktor Frankel meant when he defined emotional anguish as absolutizing your values, was that if you take the sacredness out of your values you will take much undue emotional disturbance out of your life.

If this realignment of thought, whereby you keep your preferences but unshackle your demands and stick with your wants but choke off your have tos, is so simple and beneficial, why do so few people do so? REBT theory suspects that humans are born bigots and have strong tendencies to think in black-or-white, all-or-nothing ways. Fessing up to bigotry is not an easy thing. It seems easier to blame factors of upbringing, or societal or other outside forces for one's upsets. There is more than one way to look at things, and it is often true that hardly anything is so powerful as an idea whose time has arrived. That idea could very well be that "nothing in life has to be."

Put that possibility to the acid test by making a conscious effort to curtail your dictates for the next few days. When you catch yourself proclaiming a "have to," a "must," a "should," an "ought to," or a "got to," change that declaration to a "want to," "prefer to," "desire to," "hope to," or "wish to" and find out for yourself if by nondemanding you are not less wanting for emotional relief!

Note. From *Feeling Right When Things Go Wrong* by Bill Borcherdt. Copyright © 1998, Professional Resource Exchange, Inc., P.O. Box 15560, Sarasota, FL 34277-1560.

Dime a Dozen:
Unsolicited Advisements
As Lead Balloons

"Don't put words in my mouth" is a battle cry that often goes unheard. Efforts to try to be a hero with another's problems are the rule rather than the exception. Yet, such other-directed heroics practically always fall on deaf ears. In fact, I am hard put to recall a difficult life circumstance where unasked-for direction got off the ground. This guide will explore why it's easy to be a hero with someone else's problems, why such efforts consistently falter, and how to avoid this free advice pitfall.

Unsolicited advice is easier to give than it is to follow. Here lies the main reason it is given to begin with. Suggesting to others ideas on how to better act upon their problems affords the luxury of free advice without being required to carry forth with the effort necessary to complete the suggestions. It is easier to tolerate the dirty work that someone else will be required to do to implement your noble advice. Alfred Adler stated that it's easier to fight for your ideals than to live up to them. Likewise, it's easier to suggest to someone else to fight for your ideals than it would be to put them into practice yourself. Mark Twain put the idea that unsolicited pearls of wisdom are being easier to give than to follow in this way: "It's noble to be good. It's nobler to teach others to be good - and less trouble." The human tendency to make oneself allergic to the hard work required to put oneself through to achieve a given result can be perfumed by projecting onto others that which is viewed as too strenuous to apply to yourself.

Unasked-for suggestions are likely to go unheeded because they imply the following:

1. That you know more about what is best for others than they know for themselves. This conveniences resentment in that most people prefer to be asked what they think regarding solutions rather than being told what to do.
2. That the person who is on the receiving end of your bold advice is an emotional cripple who doesn't have the resources to draw helpful conclusions on his or her own. A vote of confidence in the other's problem-solving abilities is lacking and invites increased dependency, demoting rather than promoting self-confidence.
3. That you are anointed to be the top dog in a master-slave relationship by way of making decisions for others that would be better made by themselves.
4. That you feel sorry for the other. Such other-pity trappings encourage others' whimperingness and discourages their motivation.
5. That you can discover other peoples' values for them. Lacking humility for what you can and cannot do for others will result in confusion and frustration - like trying to sell them a used car that they haven't asked for.
6. That you are scolding others for not being able to fight their own values battles in a way that you presume they can't. No one likes their hand slapped. When you butt in and try to draw conclusions for others that only they can draw for themselves, appearances of a reprimand are given off. This encourages the other to oppose you and your alleged excellent advice further.

To avoid provoking others with your gratis suggestions, consider the following suggestions:

1. Honestly track down your irrational ideas that take you to the brink of your unsolicited propositions. These might include:

   - "I know what is best for others and I just have to tell them."
   - "How ignorant of him to steer off course. I must muster up all the missionary zeal I can to show him how foolish he is (and how ingenious I am)."
   - "I'm responsible for finding solutions to my loved ones' problems and disturbances. Whether she asks for my grand advice is beside the point."
   - "My poor associate advises himself so poorly; because I can't bear to see him suffer, I am compelled to jump in and try to save him from himself."
   - "She needs to be shaken from her decision-making slumber, and I am just the person to wake her up; then she can smell the petunias. After all, I have been christened with special knowledge that she doesn't have and I'd best inform her of my anointments, poor soul."
   - "It's going to be harder for me to give this advice than it is going to be for him to follow it. It's a hard job, but somebody has to do it."
   - "I rightly pride myself in knowing more about what is best for other people than they know themselves, and I cannot in good conscience not share my free gift with them."
   - "I need to be in control of others' destiny by directing their lives, because they might make decisions that would disappoint or disadvantage me - and I could not stand such handicaps."

- "Everybody should have a Good Samaritan on their side. How fortunate others are to have a general manager of their choices like me - and all without even asking. I'm a good, better, nobler person when I give good, better, nobler advisements."

2. Counter and replace these falsehoods with the following beliefs based on the idea that "I'll run my life and not barge in and try to prevent others from running theirs."

- "There is no evidence to prove that I am more knowledgeable about other people's lives than they are."
- "Nowhere is it written that I am responsible for others' problems and upsets, that others' problems have to have an ideal solution, or that I have to find one."
- "One of the key ways to help my associates is to ask them what direction *they* think would be best for them to take - not tell them what direction I think would be best."
- "Telling others how to run their life borders on proving myself at their expense; best I try to win friends and influence others' ideas by being myself."
- "It may seem easy in the short run to try and be a hero regarding someone else's predicaments, but it will distance people in the long run because no one likes to be around a know-it-all."
- "Who am I trying to kid? Unasked-for advice is like giving someone a limp hand - it will not be taken with any degree of conviction."
- "Others will do better to live and learn from their experience, not from my almighty suggestions."
- "No one has ever invented a way to sell a used car or idea to someone who hasn't asked for one - and it is highly unlikely that I will be the first to break this impossible dream barrier."

- "Others have a right to be wrong and to learn from the consequences of their decisions. If I take it upon my heroic self to attempt to deprive them of their free will, I will only invite confusion and conflict."
- "I don't have to control anyone, and when I attempt to with my freebie suggestions, I put pressure on the both of us."
- "I don't let people make their own decisions; my choice is whether I am going to try to intercept their choice and hassle them for making it."

3. Ask not tell. By asking others what their intentions are rather than telling them what they "should," "must," or "ought to" be you are being more supportive of their problem-solving potential.

4. Walk a mile in the other's moccasins. Backtrack to a time when you were interrupted by a nagging dissenter while you were en route to making an independent judgment. Experience the annoyance that you felt while someone was inferring that he or she knew more about what was better for you than you did. Then, do unto the other what he or she would in likelihood have you do unto him or her; that is, restrain yourself from putting your nose someplace where it doesn't belong.

5. Get the green light before proceeding. Make sure the other is looking for what you are eager to provide. Confirming that another is seeking what you are eagerly wishing to provide better ensures a more receptive audience. Without this go-ahead, your well-intended suggestion will not be backed by the right, prior-authorized method and is likely to fall on deaf ears. Asking "Would you be interested in some of my thoughts on the matter?" will give your words more impact than "First I'll tell you my ideas about the problem - and then I'll tell you yours."

6. Disclaim your comfort zone as an excuse. Directly examine the possibility of your primary motives as being to

coat and perfume your own discomfort. Oftentimes, uncalled-for advice is given more for the indulgence of the sender than for the benefit of the receiver. Feelings of other-pity, superiority, smugness, or anxiety about another's discomfort can be vented through and camouflaged by unsolicited advice. To make sure that your intentions pass inspection, honestly ask yourself not so much "What advice do I want to give?" but "Why do I want to give it?" See if what is seen by way of apparent good advice is what you get by way of good reasons for giving it.

The lead balloons of unsolicited advice are a heavy burden for the sender, who is likely to find that they don't get through to his or her targeted recipient; for the receiver, who is likely to create feelings of resentment for being spoon-fed answers that he or she did not ask for; and for the relationship of the sender and receiver, that is likely to be strained by the frustrations of each. Solicited corrections are one thing; unsolicited answers are quite another. Without a green light, you are likely to jump traffic and cause an accident. So too in relationships, it is likely to be better to obtain authorization prior to unleashing advisements. Save your good advice for use in your own life, unless first requested. Model it for the other. Experience the depth of difficulty it is to follow compared to the ease of giving it. Talk is cheap. Appreciating the realities of inexpensive and easy talk will perhaps be the major encouragements to not letting yourself be so quick to ground yourself with the cheaper-by-the-dozen lead balloons of unasked-for assistance.

Note. From *Feeling Right When Things Go Wrong* by Bill Borcherdt. Copyright © 1998, Professional Resource Exchange, Inc., P.O. Box 15560, Sarasota, FL 34277-1560.

Self-Confidence
Versus
Performance Confidence:
Is What You See
Really What You Get?

The cartoon character Ziggy's psychiatrist said to him, "You're making progress in overcoming your inferiority complex - though I must say, it's the slowest progress I have ever seen." The psychiatrist was saying one thing but putting more emphasis on meaning another. Often people work on overcoming their inferiority complex by pushing themselves to perform at an exceptional level. Such strenuous efforts, although sometimes leading to high-level performances, (a) unlike Ziggy, result not only in slow progress in conquering feelings of inferiority, but no progress, and (b) like Ziggy's psychiatrist, what you see (the stated improvement) is not what you get (the actual message). Similarly, when working against diminished feelings of self, what seems to be high achievement does not always turn out to be greater self-confidence.

It seems ironic that those who excel in their specialized field of endeavor may be insecure. In fact, the more intensity of effort that is put forth, the greater may be the depth of insecurity. One would think that the baseball player who hits fifty home runs a year, the actor who stars on Broadway, or anyone else who reaches the top in their vocation would be brimming with self-confidence. Devotion to climbing the ladder of success can be done for the right reasons and for the wrong reasons. When done as a preference, for nonego reasons, it can produce vital meaning and absorption. When it is done, as is more often the case, as a demand and for ego-protecting motives, such efforts will go on endlessly as a futile effort to fill the bottomless pit of self-proving.

Lack of self-confidence is perhaps the most common human problem. What most people mean when they state they lack self-confidence is that they have a fear of failure. They view failure as bigger than life and the worst of all possible crimes and lack confidence in their ability to cope with and to accept themselves in spite of it. They then go about the business of trying to deodorize their fear by busting a gut to avoid it at all costs. What they then discover is that self-confidence is rooted in a philosophy, not in an outcome; in self-accepting, not in self-proving; and not in how well you do, but in what you tell yourself while you do it.

Self-confidence and performance or achievement confidence comes from your way of looking at life generally and your ideas about succeeding or failing specifically. These are the ways performance-confident and self-confident individuals separately size up possibilities of success and failure.

PERFORMANCE CONFIDENCE BELIEFS	SELF-CONFIDENCE PHILOSOPHIES
"I have to succeed and I have to do so no matter what. For me to fail would be disastrous and belittling. For others to notice my blunder would be doubly earth-shaking and degrading. Such humiliation I could not stand. To avoid these awful outcomes I must unmercifully push myself to succeed. That way I can prove to myself and the world that I'm not a no-good person after all."	"I want to do well, and I think there is a reasonable possibility that I can. If I would fail that would not sit well by me and I might feel disappointment. Also, if I fall short of the mark, others might take note and be quick to criticize me for my public blunder. That too would not be appreciated, but I wouldn't have to catastrophize about or condemn myself because of their prickly comments."
"If I faulted I would have to blame myself."	"I don't have to blame myself for anything, including my faults."

PERFORMANCE CONFIDENCE BELIEFS *(Cont'd)*	SELF-CONFIDENCE PHILOSOPHIES *(Cont'd)*
"It is necessary to succeed at life's projects."	"It is nice to succeed at life's projects."
"Failing is shameful."	"There is nothing under the sun to shame myself about."
"Certain happenings like failure automatically demean you."	"Demeaningness is a state of mind, and nobody or nothing can give you a state of mind."
"I have to do the perfect best in whatever I do or else I'm perfectly worthless."	"I can try to do well and remain an imperfect human being."
"I have a first-class reputation that I must live up to; to not be able to hold my own at the top of the ladder would be shattering."	"Second fiddle would not mean second class; in fact, there are no classes when it comes to humans' value to themselves."
"I have to prove myself."	"I can perhaps do better by improving my performance."
"Exceptionalism is sacred."	"Trying to do better is a credible thing to do."
"I have to do the best."	"I want to do well."
"What will people think if I fail?"	"People will think whatever they want to think about whatever I do."
"The more advantages I gain from my successes, the better person I will be."	"Any advantages I gain from my successes will make me better off, but a better person I will never be."
"The more pressure that I put on myself to succeed, the better."	"The more pressure I put on myself to succeed, the more I will clumsily unnerve myself, making it likely that I will succeed about as much as a bull in a china shop."

PERFORMANCE CONFIDENCE BELIEFS *(Cont'd)*	SELF-CONFIDENCE PHILOSOPHIES *(Cont'd)*
"Public acclaim is at the center of what really matters in life."	"Public recognition can be a great thing, but there are a million and one if not more other great things in life to enjoy."
"If I don't put all my success eggs in one basket I might never fill the basket and end up gaining nothing."	"If I put all my success eggs in one basket I might break the basket and end up losing practically everything."

As can be seen from these contrasting philosophies, what you see by way of exceptional performance is often not what you get by way of self-confidence and self-acceptance. Rather:

1. *What you see is fearlessness; what you get is fearfulness.* Performance confidence betrays the underlying fear and portrays a view that failure is shattering and therefore to be avoided at all costs.
2. *What you see is superiority; what you get is inferiority.* Performance confidence-acting people feel inferior to begin with and are really a pathetic sight in their efforts to disguise their self-belittlements by their accomplishments. They judge themselves by their work, and their superior performances are woeful attempts to perfume their feelings of inferiority.
3. *What you see is invulnerability; what you get is vulnerability.* Excelling may indicate high physical stamina, but it often reflects low emotional muscle. Achievement confidence-oriented people appear to be an island unto themselves, but their happiness is blunted due to their making themselves vulnerable to others' acceptance and approval. Contrary to steady outward appearances, they are a wobbly little boy in a big man's pants or a shaky little girl in a big girl's blouse.

4. *What you see is strength and resolve; what you get is weakness and panic.* Strong and firm is the appearance, weak and anxious is the reality experience of achievement confidence. Flooding themselves with anxiety about the possibility of failure, the performers try to stem the tide of their discomfort by demanding success.

5. *What you see is independence and self-reliance; what you get is dependence and other-directedness.* High achievers may appear to be an island unto themselves, but inwardly they make themselves dependent on others' liking and try to use their hard-pressed successes to gain such favoritism.

6. *What you see is deliberation; what you get is desperation.* Performance confidence appears to be calculated and deliberate, but this is a front for overconcern over the prospect of what others might think about you in observing your flub.

7. *What you see is peace and personal fulfillment; what you get is inner turmoil and personal unhappiness.* Because motivation by self-proving is an endless project, the self-prover never gets around to more fully accepting himself or herself and remains chronically frustrated.

Confucius said, "To go beyond is as wrong as to fall short." Perfect your attempts to perform and achieve without burdening yourself with the impossible dream of being perfect. Don't bust your rump in an effort to prove you're superhuman. Leave your fear of failure and disapproval anxiety at the doorstep. Approach, if not attack, your ambitions in a clearheaded, well-thought-out, permissive way where you allow yourself some emotional slack. Heed Confucius' advice to not try to go beyond what is humanly possible. That way you will be more likely to not fall short of what is humanly possible. Then, what you see by way of confidently performing will be what you get by way of self-confidence.

Note. From *Feeling Right When Things Go Wrong* by Bill Borcherdt. Copyright © 1998, Professional Resource Exchange, Inc., P.O. Box 15560, Sarasota, FL 34277-1560.

From Rags to Riches: Avoiding the Disadvantages of Advantages

Oscar Wilde said, "In this world there are only two trage-dies. One is not getting what one wants, and the other is getting it." Mother Theresa put it differently: "More tears come from answered than unanswered prayers." According to these two perspectives, being rich apparently has as many problems as being poor. Growing up on the right side of the tracks is as likely to have as many disappointments as growing up on the wrong side. Hassles, imperfections, deprivations, and inconveniences will not vanish just because you get your heart's desire, because your prayers turn into realities, or be-cause you can afford to move from one side of the tracks to the other.

Strive for your goals but don't buffalo yourself into be-lieving that a chance or planned change of scenery will be the ultimate answer to life's dissatisfactions. Keep that far-from-the-truth pipe dream far out of your mind. Upon approaching and when achieving a long-sought-after goal, one often is ill-prepared to deal with the tarnish on it. The solution often brings problems. One measure of success is how it is dealt with. This guide will identify the pitfalls of gaining your heart's desire and what can be done to cushion the reality of something bad in something good. Gaps in expectations versus realities are more the rule than the exception. Reality often kills the dream. Whether it be finally marrying the love of your life, getting a job that seems to fit you to a T, completing a longstanding project, or winning the trophy or prize that you have long prepared yourself to compete for, the actual experience of becoming the victor often falls short of original anticipations.

Bracing yourself for the following possible negative consequences of success can ward off the disillusionment that comes from embracing pie-in-the-sky, rags-to-riches assumptions.

1. *Idle time.* What to do now that you have done what you have mainly wanted to do is not always an easy answer. Being preoccupied with the road to success may leave you at a loss as to how to structure your time after you get to success.

2. *Emotional emptiness.* A sense of anticipation and participation goes along with tracking burning desires. Once the cutting edge of mental sharpness is lost following success, the fire of competitive keenness is often allowed to burn out.

3. *Higher expectations from others.* Once you achieve the margin of victory, others may expect even bigger and better things from you in the future. This may conflict with your own desire to enjoy your achievement rather than seek more.

4. *Invasion of privacy.* Once you establish yourself as a success in your field, others may inconveniently insist on a piece of the action. Consequently, your life may become overprogrammed, leaving you little time for simple enjoyments.

5. *Loss of the good old days.* Many who make it to the top in their field look back longingly to the time when they could mix business and pleasure more on their terms, away from the "madding crowd," with the luxury of their own pace of anticipation. In retrospect, humble beginnings are often seen as not being all that bad when stacked against the present complications of success.

6. *Fish-out-of-water discomforts.* Unfamiliar territory often breeds discomfort. Until you get used to your successful station, it may seem out of character and awkward. The promised land often isn't all you promised yourself about feeling great once you arrived.

7. *Others' skepticism and criticism.* Successful people are often the envy of others who may doubt the deservingness of your successes and make it a point to find flaws in your accomplishments. The more successful you are, the more interpersonal problems you may run into about your successes.

8. *Looking over your shoulder.* Satchel Paige said, "Don't look back. Something might be gaining on you." Worries about being knocked off your perch create suspicions that someone may be catching up to you. Hearing such footsteps prevents you from enjoying your successes.

9. *How soon they forget.* Abundant praise may be an immediate reward for success. An emotional letdown can result when such positive reinforcement runs out shortly after the showing is over.

10. *Temptations of uppityness.* Doing better does not make you a better person. Due to human tendencies to rate themselves, one can easily muscle oneself into a psychological one-upmanship stance: "If I do better than you, I am better than you."

11. *Fear of appearing uppity.* Overconcerning yourself about leaving an impression on others that you think you are better than they are will result in you falling all over yourself with the next potential disadvantage of hitting your mark.

12. *Nauseating humility.* Apologizing for your successes distracts from the pleasure of them as well as from the pleasure of your company.

13. *Others' avoidance.* Others less successful than you may not only rate themselves as inferior to you, but out of their insecurity avoid your association due to its reminders of their negative self-view.

Alas, success doesn't have to be hazardous to your health. The following suggestions will take you beyond the turmoil and conflict related to finding what you seek.

1. *Expect less.* Acknowledging beforehand that getting your heart's desire will not spring eternal happiness will prevent much heartache and headache.

2. *Promote a philosophy of ongoingness.* View life and happiness as a continuing process, not a place you arrive and rest on the remainder of your time. Such an ongoing view will keep you going in an invigorating manner.

3. *Inventory other pursuits and mastery activities.* Don't concentrate exclusively on the one goal on the front burner. Keep replacement goals on the back burner for use when you see fit to interject fresh meaning into your life.

4. *Avoid deification and devilification of self and others.* Don't play the rating game where you give yourself and others a report card with a good mark because of your advantages and a bad mark due to disadvantages. You and others actively participate in your advantages or disadvantages, but you are not them. You and they are better off with advantages and worse off without them, but not a better or worse person.

5. *Make yourself less reinforceable.* To make yourself dependent on praise following successes limits your ability to enjoy them in that favorable attention for your accomplishments follows the pattern of today's hero as tomorrow's forgotten person - and how soon they forget!

6. *Relinquish compliment phobia.* Get yourself past the shy, sheepish feelings that accompany an overconcern about appearing too brash when others acknowledge your success. How others interpret your acceptance of their praise is out of your hands.

7. *Cultivate more of an immunity to criticism.* The bigger a success you are, the harder others sometimes would like to see you fall. Train yourself to limit tendencies to overreact to, and define yourself by, others' barbs.

8. *See that happiness is an inside job.* Inner peace does not rely on outer accomplishments. Happiness is more related to your philosophy about life than to your successes in it. Mainly, happiness is a direct ratio between what you expect and what you get. The more realistic you are as to what to expect from successful outcomes, the happier you will be.

9. *Concentrate more on the business at hand.* Focus more on what you are doing now in attending to your projects and less on the future outcomes of your labor. With fewer future expectations, you will be less likely to "awfulize" at one extreme or "wonderfulize" at the other.

10. *Inform others along the way.* Telling others about what you are finding in your goal-seeking efforts and what you expect to find can be helpful in organizing an understanding that minimizes the gap between what you expect today and what you get tomorrow. Knowing others will be interested in the outcome of your predictions can help to keep you more realistically targeted.

11. *Set limits on yourself.* The desire of others that you bust a gut so you can continue to produce doesn't mean that you have to. Be your own person following achievements by being selective about how long and how hard you want to keep up the beat of your efforts. The fact that you once paid the price of success doesn't mean you have to continue to extend yourself, especially if such strenuous efforts would be against your healthful interests.

12. *Understand that you can run but you can't hide.* Especially if you are making yourself miserable about present adversities, see that even if you get yourself to a more favorable station in life, you are likely to carry with you the same view you had in your misery. Change your misery-producing thinking about your disadvantages before you attempt to change unwanted conditions more to your liking. Otherwise, you will make yourself unhappy all over again once reality abolishes the dream.

Regardless of what side of the fence you are on, life is not a bowl of cherries. When current objectives expire, have in hand heart and head replacement goals and replace low tolerance and nonaccepting attitudes with views that permit a more realistic understanding of the human condition. Move into success in your chosen field of interest but do so with your eyes wide open. Though success is frequently not all it's cracked up to be, this doesn't mean you can't avoid many of its trappings. Avoid a letdown by letting yourself understand that people can be rich in proportion to what they can afford to go without as well as what they believe within.

Use of Force and Enforcement In Countering With Fuller Force Emotional Upset

When individuals produce their own emotional disturbance they very powerfully tell themselves irrational ideas to do so. Here is a sampling of disturbance-producing beliefs:

- "It's horrible others are treating me badly!"
- "I can't stand feeling uncomfortable!"
- "How awful that injustice exists!"
- "What a failure I am for failing!"
- "I shouldn't be required to do things that I don't want to do!"
- "I must solve my problems!"
- "What a louse I am for coping so poorly!"
- "I can't bear feeling so upset!"
- "What an ass I am for acting so asininely!"
- "What an ass you are for acting so asininely!"

In each example an explanation point is used to illustrate the strength of the belief. Therefore, when countering emotional upset, it is important to more than equally as strongly argue against your nonsense. Just as how you talk to others affects them, how you talk to yourself affects you. It is not just what you say, but how intensely you say it. Having knowledge of rational coping ideas is one thing, reviewing them with yourself is another, and doing so in a pronounced, vigorous manner is most important if your goal is to enforce them by acting upon them. My clients report that simply reviewing rational ideas is helpful at a light to moderate level. Energetically and passionately self-stating them is reported to bring fuller meaning, leading to the action component of problem solving. The "E" in REBT (rational emotive behavior therapy) is there for a reason: to emphasize the *emotive, energetic, exciting, exhilarating* component of human existence. Use this forceful component of human emotion and behavior to convince yourself of rational ideas that reflect increased tolerance and acceptance, en route to behavior change.

There seems to be a real bias in problem solving toward calmness, relaxation, and serenity. I think such comfort-junkie leanings are in error in that most of what has been accomplished by way of human endeavor met requirements of vigor, force, energy, and passion - not hypnotic, laid-back living. Comfort has its appeal, but when it comes to something worth achieving, a more dramatic, no-nonsense effect had best be brought - if not pushed - into play. "Insight," or understanding what you are disturbed about, is not enough to improve your plot, though it alone is often considered to be the ultimate goal of present-day problem solving. Strongly disputing irrational beliefs is more likely to generate the momentum required to get behind yourself and determinedly push yourself onto the field of action. A philosophy of sustained effort to the task at hand is more likely to come from a toned-up tone of voice. You may be saying all the right rational things to yourself, but unless you say them with a strong emphasis it is unlikely that you will muster up enough strength of your convictions to create a more nonavoidant approach to life.

So, say it with meaning! Forcefully encounter and counter your self-defeating ideas, using some of these disturbance-removing statements and disputations as references to draw from:

- "Why is it so horrible when others are treating me badly?"

- "I may not like feeling uncomfortable, but I can certainly stand it!"
- "Injustice is a disappointing reality that I would do well to accept!"
- "I do my failures, but I am not my failures!"
- "Where is the evidence that I shouldn't be required to do things that I don't want to do?"
- "I would like to solve my problems, but, as a flawed human being, it is likely that there will be many I will be unable to solve!"
- "When I cope lousily, I am not a louse!"
- "I don't like making myself feel so upset, but I can tolerate what I don't like in this or any other instance!"
- "I am not an ass for acting asininely!"
- "Others are not asses for acting asininely!"

Humans bring themselves to their feelings and behaviors by their guiding thoughts. Find the rational beliefs that will better contribute to your emotional and behavioral wellness and strongly instill them into your worldview. A Buddhist philosophy states, "To know and not to use is the same as not to know." Knowledge is not the same as action; attempted empowerment without vigorous emotive backups will likely leave you glossing over, once over lightly, important pieces of knowledge. Use of this knowledge is preceded by strongly knowing and convincing yourself of its substance. What you say to yourself and how you say it largely determines what you do with your life. If your goal is to do more doing and less drifting, counter your mistaken ideas with fuller force and see if this does not lead to you achieving your fuller potential.

Note. From *Feeling Right When Things Go Wrong* by Bill Borcherdt. Copyright © 1998, Professional Resource Exchange, Inc., P.O. Box 15560, Sarasota, FL 34277-1560.

The Ultraconformist And the Nagging Dissenter: Similar Hearses With Different License Plates

Ultraconformists and nagging dissenters have in common taking their cue from others. The conformist looks at what everybody else is thinking and doing and thinks and repeatedly does the same thing. The dissenter observes others' thoughts and actions and equally as unthinkingly follows suit with opposing ideas and actions. Like the man in the gray flannel suit of the 1950s who worshipped sameness, and the beatniks of the 1960s who made being different sacred, individuality and self-choosing are lost in these other-directed approaches. Each comes to their life situations with a rigid view that determines what they will conclude about it and how they will conduct themselves in it, rather than more open-mindedly deciding after weighing the presenting factors.

Clients who put themselves on this for-or-against, automatic-pilot response often tell me that they are not aware of any thoughts that they have just before they respond in such a repeated way. "I didn't think anything - I just did it" is a frequent comment. What I then try to explain is that like practically all humans, they likely have preconceived ideas about what certain situations mean for them. Then, when these circumstances arise, these predetermined notions are kicked into gear in a semi-automatic way. People become so well practiced in their self-statements that they are not aware that they are there. People put themselves into an invisible straitjacket that causes them to become a slave to unexamined beliefs. Making yourself aware of the false notions that create this self-imposed emotional bandage is the first step toward unshackling yourself from it. This guide will address the black-and-white, all-or-nothing thinking that lurks behind these contrasting outlooks and what can be done to avoid the similar disadvantages that exclusive conformity or dissent brings.

Examples of ultraconformity include:

- Constantly agreeing with something just because someone said it.
- Going to a place of religious worship because others do rather than because you want to.
- Honoring someone's request because others before you have.
- Voting on an issue or for a candidate because all others in your social group did.
- Cutting your grass because your neighbors did.
- Sending your child to a certain school just because your friends or relatives did.
- Contributing to the United Fund because everyone else at work did and not because you sincerely wanted to contribute to that group.
- Joining a club because most others you know have.
- Getting married because all your friends are.
- Consistently expressing yourself about topics to meet with the pleasure of the group and not because you really believe your position.
- Getting yourself angry about a concern just because others are.
- Asserting yourself because others might criticize you if you don't.
- Crying at a funeral simply because others are.
- Selecting against and criticizing others mainly because those around you are.

- Attending a family or class reunion not because you want to but because most others you know are.
- Acting sad or depressed some time after a loss not because you truly are but because you believe it to be the expected thing to do.
- Asking (or not asking) a question just because others in the group or class are (or aren't).
- Indulging in alcohol or illicit drugs not because you have a yearning to do so but because you will likely be mocked by your associates if you don't.
- Dressing the way you do so you "fit in" to current fashion rather than because you appreciate the trend.
- Participating in self-development programs such as assertion, meditation, and adult children of alcoholic meetings, and reading popular psychology books not because you think they may prove helpful to you, but because most others in your immediate social circle are.

Illustrations of nagging dissension are:

- Listening close to what the Republican speaker has to say so that you can build a case for the Democratic position (or visa versa).
- Paying close attention to what someone states about a social or religious issue for the sole purpose of refuting it.
- Wearing your hair long (short) because most others are wearing it short (long).
- Becoming a vegetarian because most people aren't.
- Supporting an unpopular cause just to annoy others.
- Sending your child to a private school because no one else in the neighborhood is.
- Dressing outlandishly simply to bring attention to yourself.

- Boycotting a social function mainly to find out if those who went noticed you were absent.
- Purposefully not expressing the mood of the group as an insistence that you be different.
- Acting boldly assertive because no one else is.
- Living well below your means as a way to draw attention to yourself in that those in your socioeconomic status don't.
- Not getting married because most others you know are.
- Saying "no" ("yes") largely because others expect you to say "yes" ("no").
- Acting contrary for the sole purpose of countering others' pleasantries.
- Sacrificing yourself for a cause because you note hardly anyone else is.
- Voting for an unpopular candidate just to contradict your social group's consensus.
- Staying late at work in purposeful response to all others in your work group leaving on the hour.

Whether intentionally doing what others are doing or purposefully not doing what others are doing, your own seal of approval is not stamped on your efforts. In leaving others' mark and not your own on your decision, you make yourself out to act like a trained seal. Such an outer-directed manner blocks and betrays your own values realization. Confusion, uncertainty, and feelings of emptiness are a consequence of your self-choosing hesitations. Such emotional flounderings are against the goals of rational living - to extend and develop yourself to your fuller potential.

In all these illustrations, it is not the behavior itself that is for or against your best interests. Rather, the problem is the prior rigid, mechanical, pigeon-hole thinking that, left unchallenged, leads you to your tunnel-vision choices. It is not what you decide but the extreme versus the more well-thought-out manner in which you decide that had best be examined. There are common and uncommon denominators to both the inflexible and flexible sides of the ledger. The ultraconformist, nagging dissenter, and rational perspectives will now be reviewed in terms of general principles, precise self-sentences, emotional outcomes, and practical disadvantages or advantages.

1. *Perspective:* Ultraconformist.

General principles involved:

- Makes self emotionally dependent on others' acceptance and approval
- Fears own discomforts related to distinguishing self from others
- Worships sameness and despises differences
- Reeks with all-or-nothing thinking
- Sees things as black or white
- Views failure as shattering
- Easily shames self
- Takes criticism exceptionally personally
- Believes others' opinions represent him or her
- Exaggerates the significance of appearing different

Precise irrational self-sentences:

- "I have to be like everybody else - or else I'm nobody."
- "I can't stand appearing different from the majority."
- "The majority is always right and good."
- "I feel too unbearably out of sorts when I stand out like a sore thumb."
- "Others will think less of me if I don't form an alliance with them - and that would be terrible."

- "If I'm going to get anyplace in life, I have to march to the tune of everybody else's drummer."
- "I need others to think well of me, and the only way to do this is to be just like them."

Emotional outcome:

- Disapproval anxiety
- Fear
- Discomfort anxiety
- Worry
- Shame

Practical disadvantages:

- Learns little as associates mainly with those who think alike
- Easily falls into a rut
- Experiences less variety and spark in interpersonal relationships
- Misses out on many experiences due to avoidance philosophy
- Experiences more stress symptoms due to pressure put on self to conform
- Performs inefficiently because of tension build-up

2. *Perspective:* Nagging dissenter.

General principles involved:

- Makes self emotionally dependent on opposing others' views
- Acts superior to conceal that he or she secretly feels inferior
- Likes playing psychological one-upmanship
- Has conflicts with authority

- Has a fanatical and controlling nature
- Has deficiencies of empathy and tactfulness
- Uses controversy and oppositionalism to combat boredom and/or depression
- Has grandiosity (believes he or she is the center of the universe)
- Is demanding by nature
- Worships attention
- Lacks compassion for others
- Dramatizes the significance of others disobeying his or her values
- Has characteristics of self-centeredness and narrow-mindedness
- Holds extremist philosophies

Precise irrational self-sentences:

- "I have to appear different from others."
- "I must prove my absolute superiority over others by defining myself as extremely different from them."
- "Life is boring unless I do things drastically different."
- "Society and authority have no right to thwart and balk my freedoms - I'll show them who is boss."
- "What a great feeling to be at the center of controversy; I couldn't stand it any other way."
- "I know what is better for the masses than they do."
- "If everyone would think like me, instead of opposing me, the world would be such a better place instead of the pitiful way it is now."

Emotional Outcome:

- Anger
- Anguish
- Rage
- Fury

Practical disadvantages:

- Drives others away as they turn against him or her
- Learns little because spends so much time by self
- Performs poorly due to pressure put on self to prove self
- Experiences social isolation from acting like a porcupine
- Has symptoms of stress and tension related to futile efforts to make over the universe and others in it

3. *Perspective:* The rational-acting person.

General principles involved:

- Practices philosophies of tolerance and undamning acceptance
- Makes decisions by preference rather than demand
- Builds a case for deliberation rather than desperation
- Forgoes self and other judgments
- Seeks to develop high, rather than giving himself or herself low, frustration tolerance
- Seeks neither to habitually conform nor to oppose but to be himself or herself in lieu of proving himself or herself
- Establishes what he or she truly wants to do rather than arbitrarily define what he or she "should," "must," or "ought" to do
- Develops balance and rotation in contacts with his or her social group

Precise rational self-sentences:

- "Though I find it great to be on the receiving end of others' acceptance and approval, such favoritisms are hardly necessary."

- "Being out of step with group consensus certainly has its discomforts, but this is a small price to pay for avoiding nauseating conformity."
- "Purposefully being different may highlight my views and bring me more group recognition, but practicing extremism to get my point across is not necessary and in the long run is likely to result in others paying more attention to my drama than my message."
- "Agreeing or disagreeing with others does not make me a better person, only a person who agrees or disagrees. In fact, to the best of scientific knowledge, nothing makes me a better (or worse) person."
- "Sometimes the majority is right, sometimes the minority is; no one has a monopoly on truth."
- "It is likely to be in my long-range best interest if I consistently march to the tune of my own, rather than the same or a different, drummer."
- "I can stand the discomforts of being different as well as the boredom sometimes associated with sameness."
- "It is unlikely that others know what is best for me or that I know what is best for them. All of us would do well to read the handwriting on the wall and decide what would appear to be better for each of us, at this time, in this circumstance."

Emotional outcome:

- Feelings of relief
- More clearheadedness
- High frustration tolerance
- Stress- and tension-less living

Practical advantages:

- Decisive decision making
- Better concentration leading to more efficient problem solving

- More informality and give and take with your social group
- Increased skill development due to your ability to focus on your more clear-cut, independent choices, and time saving because you hedge less on what is best for you

Make up your own mind! March to the tune of your own drummer! Avoid the social extremist positions of insisting on being on the inside looking out or on the outside looking in. The conformist who deifies agreement and the dissenter who makes controversy sacred are, in their contrasting ways, assuring their being on time for their own funeral. Such a similar yet different collision course can be avoided. Most people concentrate on their circumstances rather than their thinking about it to explain their emotions. Yet, the stimulus doesn't cause the response. Humans are not trained seals and are not required to respond automatically to external events. They can instead make allowances and favor their best interests by picking and choosing those responses that would best suit them. I believe it was the philosopher Nietzsche who said, "If the only tool you have is a hammer, you will treat everything as if it were a nail." Why nail shut your own emotional coffin by standardizing your philosophies of life? Would it not be better to be more permissive in your views? That way you can avoid living or dying by someone else's directive and instead lead a more self-choosing, varied, and interesting life.

Whys and Wherefores: Eight Reasons To Avoid Paralysis of the Analysis

Did the devil really make me do it, was it the result of some sort of unconscious slippage, or was it long past family-of-origin experiences that tipped the scales in the direction of self-defeating behavior? Humans have a marked tendency to use magic, vagueness, and past experiences to explain themselves in relationship to their current upsets. These alleged movers of today's emotional predicaments muddy the problem-solving waters, cause one to overlook more accessible ideas with which to develop oneself, and serve as a distraction from more direct, responsible means of self-help.

Humans tend to have a love affair with unknown quantities to explain their plight. "Why did I do that?" "What caused me to act that way?" "Why did I make this decision and not a better one?" "Insight" as a way to explain one's behavior is often seen as the ultimate method of problem solving. Such alleged understandings do not have magical corrective measures attached to them. They do provide short-range comforts and conveniences that go along with leading oneself to believe that understanding is an end in itself. However, an analysis of background factors that presumably color one's behavior has the following disadvantages:

1. *Encourages passive rather than active means of problem solving.* The search for special reasons behind your conduct conveniences such detective work to become an end in itself.

2. *Hinders acknowledgment of accountability.* Self-responsibility can easily be given a back seat in a search for background factors to explain the facts of your life.

3. *Lets the obvious escape.* Humans are accidents looking and waiting for a place to happen. They come into the world remarkably fallible. They are demanders and over-reactors by nature rather than nurture. They have pre-existing tendencies to trouble themselves and look for and find situations to give vent to their imperfections. To look for special reasons "why" humans act in problematic ways is to look for a needle in a haystack that doesn't exist.

4. *Rationalizes inaction.* Believing that personal change can only be accomplished with a thorough analysis of the matter will likely lead to putting on hold the perspiration required to promote the problem-solving inspiration.

5. *Diverts from fuller understanding and acceptance.* Digging for the whys and wherefores of self-understanding will result in doing a little bit of a lot of things but not too much of any one thing for concentrated problem solving. Identifying and admitting to your own "upsetability" (your ability to upset yourself for no special reason) quickly sets the stage for pledging yourself to do better - with no other conditions of understanding attached. Declaring "I upset/disadvantage myself; now how can I upset/disadvantage myself less?," pure and simple, gives you immediate access to accepting and correcting your wrongdoing.

6. *Doesn't resolve the fault-versus-blame dilemma.* The search for unknown reasons for faulty choices often disguises self-blame tendencies. Feverishly looking for outside reasons for mistakes often reflects the mentality of "If I'm at fault, I am to be blamed." Understanding that blame doesn't have to be tacked on to fault will leave you less inclined to try to justify your behavior by matters beyond your control.

7. *Doesn't get you out of the comfort trap.* Immediate comfort if not indulgence is attained when curiosity about seeming determining factors becomes an end in itself. It is more comfortable to think about presumed hidden factors than it is to begin action on known quantities. A philosophy of effort is lost in the shuffle by sitting back and analyzing the situation further.

8. *Sets a precedent for bad habits.* Lulling yourself into procrastinating, avoidant patterns can be habit forming. Putting off doing today by analyzing unprovable possibilities until doomsday enforces and reinforces a casual rather than a spirited approach to coping with life's hassles.

If digging for the whys and wherefores is like panning for fool's gold, what would be wiser methods of problem solving? Getting past this cluttered, bottomless-pit manner of figuring yourself out can be done with heavy doses of consequential and rational thinking, of course! Instead of asking yourself "Why did I do that?," ask, "What were the consequences of what I did?" Then, decide for yourself whether you wish to continue to produce such results. If your behavior does not further your stated goals, you can change it in a way that may gain better results.

Rational emotive behavior therapy (REBT) includes consequential thinking while directly and quickly getting at the heart of emotional disturbance. It clearly defines emotional upset not as the devil in disguise, the result of an unconscious quirk, or created by harsh family-of-record experiences. Rather, it openly holds individuals accountable for their problems by spelling out emotional disturbance as demands placed on self, others, and the conditions of life. If individuals are feeling guilty or depressed, it is because they are putting unrealistic demands on themselves in the form of precise explanatory self-sentences such as, "I have to do perfectly well or else I'm perfectly worthless. I have to succeed in virtually all my projects and I am to down and damn myself for accomplishing anything less than hitting the perfectionistic bull's-eye!" When angry, people are likely strongly telling themselves, "You have to treat me kindly and considerately at all times - especially if I am consistently pleasant acting to you. And when you don't give me a return on my good efforts to patronize you, you are perfectly worthless and I'll damn and despise you until the day you die - and I hope it's soon!" When feeling listlessness or self-pity, one in good probability is emphatically insisting that "The conditions of life have to make it easy for me to reach my goals and confirm my ambitions, and when such convenient access is not granted, I'll whine, withdraw, and make it a special point to make myself feel undisciplined about and antagonistic toward life."

With no tricks or short-cuts, REBT defogs personal problem solving. It actively and avidly encourages its participants to challenge protests against reality, refusals to accept what exists, and exaggerations about the significance of things. It strongly advises a more accepting worldview while coaching countering declarations such as "I'm only human, not perfect - I'll do my best without insisting that I do the best!" "Although I strongly prefer kind treatment from others, there is no evidence that anyone in my social group is required to return kindness with kindness (because, after all, I don't run the universe yet)!" "It would be great if I could be anointed to be the one person in the universe to easily realize his or her ambitions, but because I'm not, best I work hard to achieve my values just like practically everyone else is required to!"

Search and research no more! Don't let the obvious escape you. When troubled, immediately identify the insistencies you are placing on yourself, others, and life. Debate and dispute them in vintage REBT fashion. Discover for yourself that you don't have to look for the whys and wherefores, needle-in-a-haystack means that are the dead-ends of paralysis-of-the-analysis problem solving.

Accepting the Bad, Yet Refuting the Good: Extracting the Ego From Compliment Phobia

It is interesting how often people won't take seriously a compliment directed their way but will take with dead-serious intent a criticism targeted for them. In that some people will like you for the same traits others dislike, sometimes the compliment or criticism is even directed toward the same characteristic by two different people! For instance, one person may applaud your sense of humor while another will downgrade it. Personalizing the negative and overlooking the positive in others' comments limits the flavor of your connections with others. Throwing cold water on the sender's affirmations is likely to contribute to alienating him or her. Criticizing another's judgment is not exactly a surefire way to win friends and influence people, nor to experience the satisfaction that comes from gaining the unsolicited approval from someone in your social group.

Statements that reflect compliment disclaimers:

- "Do you really think so?"
- "I could have done better."
- "It's really nothing."
- "It wasn't all that good."
- "I didn't think it's anything to brag about."
- "I've seen a lot, lot better."
- "You're just saying that."

- "You don't have to be so nice."
- "You're only saying that to be kind."
- "I didn't think it was good at all."
- "Even you can do better than that."
- "No one else thinks so."
- "That was terrible - how can you say I did good?"
- "Ah, come on now, who are you trying to kid? You're just trying to be nice because you want something."
- "You just want me to say something nice back to you."
- "You're just trying to embarrass me - you couldn't really mean that."
- "Aw, it wasn't anything to write home about."

Such nauseating humility is preceded by irrational ideas that prevent compliments from getting through to the refreshing point of acceptance. Likewise, when allowed to soak in, such straightforward acknowledgment is made to happen via ideas that open the rational doors of acceptance. What follows is a review of the thoughts that result in compliment denial and compliment acceptance, the reasons for each, and the consequences of the decision to not accept or to accept a compliment.

Thoughts that block compliment acceptance:

- "I secretly think I'm better than others, and if I accept others' verbal honorariums, they will know what I've been trying to hide all these years."
- "Others might think I'm uppity if I'm the least bit forward in acknowledging their good review."
- "The meek shall inherit the earth, so the meeker I act when complimented, the more power I will eventually have."
- "Others will criticize and disapprove of me if they see me buying a compliment someone else is selling. In that I need others' likings, I will bend over backwards to get it by eating humble pie when complimented."

- "I feel so sheepish when complimented, so I'll discourage others from complimenting me so as to avoid feeling so intolerably out of sorts."
- "I just know that if I accept this compliment I will be expected to give one in return. Because I always have to do what is expected of me, I won't put myself into such a duty-bound position to begin with."
- "Taking in compliments is so out of character for me and I couldn't possibly expect myself to do anything that would be out of the ordinary."
- "I've been taken in by wolves in sheep's clothing before and I'll be dipped if I will ever put myself in a position to let that happen again - I don't care how nice he or she seems."
- "I've always been taught not to appear too brassy, and I must always believe what I was taught so as to avoid the appearance of others thinking that I think I'm better than they are."
- "Knock on wood, if I acknowledge my achievements I'm liable to not be able to keep up the beat of my achievements. (Because there is something magical that will continue them if I just keep quiet about their content.)"
- "The golden rule is 'Thou shalt not appear proud and accomplished,' so I'd best honor this sacred regulation lest something bad happen to me."
- "Don't ask me where I got the idea, but I know I shouldn't go along with documenting my own accomplishments."

Reasons for compliment denial:

1. *Fear of feeling out of sorts while accepting the compliment.* Discomfort anxiety is made to be supreme by exaggerating the significance of feeling awkward in the up-front acceptance of another's pleasant comment about your project or personal characteristic.

2. *Dire needs for acceptance and approval.* Defining your-self by others' possible disapproval of your openly ac-cepting a compliment will block you from doing so.
3. *Fear of being manipulated.* Remembering that flattery has gotten others anywhere with you in the past, and fearing that accepting another's favoritism will set you up to be used again, results in a quick denial of their compli-ment.
4. *Believing that you must reciprocate.* Assuming that if someone says something nice to you, you are required to say something back will spoil your believing another's positive review.
5. *Feelings of inferiority.* Believing that because you are such a crumb you could not produce anything but crum-my accomplishments will stop you short of accepting that others could believe anything different.
6. *Feelings of superiority.* Wanting to hide your godlike ambitions is accomplished when you correct others for the merits they find in your behavior. Being in the habit of giving yourself a good, sacred report card for your appreciation of yourself can be disguised by depreciating others' wholesome comments about what they find pleas-ing about you.
7. *Voodooistic, magical thinking.* Keeping your light hidden under a bushel is deified when you believe that (a) if you let the cat out of the bag by being proud of your accom-plishments, your accomplishments will somehow cease to exist; and (b) by keeping your accomplishments hidden you are somehow guaranteeing they will continue.

Consequences of compliment rebuff:

1. *A turning away by your social group.* When you turn away a compliment you are throwing cold water on someone else's judgment. Downplaying others' views will wear down a relationship fast. Second-guessing others' tastes will likely prompt their future avoidance of

you. No one likes to bluntly be told that they are wrong, including regarding a favorable opinion about you.

2. *Loss of the energy that comes from others' emotional support.* We live in a prickly world, and you'd best not look an affirmative gift horse in the mouth. Sidestepping validations of your strengths will result in you feeling weaker.

3. *Practice in self-downing.* The belief that you are inferior and therefore not capable of anything but inferior performances gets reinforced by snubbing what someone thought was noteworthy about you.

4. *Expression and rehearsal of your other critical nature.* If you can't take a compliment without criticizing the sender, what can you take without criticizing someone? Perhaps the ultimate in other criticism is the unwillingness to graciously accept another's favorable review of your good points.

Statements that reflect an enlightened, unhedging acceptance of a compliment:

- "I appreciate your noticing."
- "That was kind of you to notice."
- "Thank you."
- "You say such nice things."
- "That was pleasant to hear."
- "It's nice to know that you noticed."
- "That was good to hear."
- "What a pleasant thing to say."
- "It feels good to hear something good."
- "What you said is valuable to me."

Thoughts that lead to compliment acceptance:

- "Granted, if I accept a compliment others might think I'm uppity, but I know that is not true, and what I think is more important than what others might think."

- "Meeker does not mean better, and eating humble pie when someone says something kind about me is definitely not to my advantage."
- "Even though at first I may feel awkward about accepting a compliment, if I keep doing it, familiarity and practice are likely to numb my terror about it."
- "Getting and accepting a compliment can be such a refreshing feeling if I let it, so what better thing to do than help myself to feel more the way I want to feel?"
- "Although it is true that some people may try to take advantage of me by showering me with compliments, I need not make myself feel hurt about such occurrences. Therefore, I can afford to trust myself and others at the same time by not prejudging them as having ulterior motives."
- "The fact that I'm not used to accepting compliments doesn't mean I can't get used to it. Any nervousness about doing it does not mean I'm a phony; rather, that is the price I pay for doing something different."
- "When I unashamedly acknowledge my achievements, I reinforce my efforts and consequently am more likely to continue to do well."
- "Because I was taught that humility is a sacred matter does not mean I have to keep that belief alive, especially if it is against my best interest to do so."
- "Others may expect to receive a compliment in return for theirs, but that does not mean I have to give one in return or that I would be banished from the human race if I didn't."

Reasons for compliment acceptance:

1. A desire to have a well-rounded relationship with one's social group. Being able to have personal agreements with others helps balance the differences that any two people naturally have.

2. Understanding that accepting what another has to say is an emotional benefit for the sender.
3. Realizing that *undependent desires* for social approval are a pleasant experience.
4. Wanting to create a more wholesome climate in your social circle by modeling how pleasant it is for both parties to comfortably give and receive a compliment.

Consequences of compliment acceptance:

1. More comparability and less conflict with your social group.
2. A strengthening of emotional ties between the sender and receiver.
3. Feelings of well-being and satisfaction in both the sender and receiver.
4. Contributions to a more affirmative social climate.

"What's the matter? Don't you know how to take a compliment?" Take the compliment and run with it - not as if your life depended on it, but because it may add something favorable to your life. Grab your best efforts and get your appreciations and leave your fears of disapproval and discomfort at the doorstep. Life can be so much sweeter if you look at the part of the bottle that is full and accept others' acclaim when they do the same.

Note. From *Feeling Right When Things Go Wrong* by Bill Borcherdt. Copyright © 1998, Professional Resource Exchange, Inc., P.O. Box 15560, Sarasota, FL 34277-1560.

The Long and Short of It: Length of Solution As Shortened from The Length of the Problem

"Because it took a long time to create a problem, it's going to take a long time to solve it" is a prediction that is commonly held by client and counselor alike. Such belief has a soft-shoe, lulling, slower-than-molasses-in-January ring to it for both consumer and service provider. This deterministic notion provides feelings of immediate comfort for the client; after all, if it's going to take a long time, why not take my time in moving away from business as usual? A smug sense of comfort and convenience is gained by proclaiming that the end to your problems is not near, so why bother to push the river? Why not instead conveniently let it flow? In knowing that he or she can retain a paying customer for a lengthy period of time, the therapist also gains a comforting sense of reassurance from this go-slowly theory. So although this self-fulfilling promise - I promise myself that because it took a long time to create the problem it's going to take a long time to solve it - pays dividends, interest in speeding up the self-help process is kept low, in the disservice of emotional well-being.

Believing that it could take a long time to solve a problem but not necessarily so leaves open the possibility of saving time, energy, and money in the business of problem solving. Such a flexible, open-minded outlook increases the chances of getting on more quickly with the enjoyments of life. There is much evidence that people are capable of learning ideas that can quickly turn their life around. There are countless people who have read a self-help book, listened to a self-improvement tape, or sat in on a 1-hour personal and/or interpersonal skills lecture and then used information learned to swiftly move themselves into a happier mode of living. One of the things that I have found most fascinating and exciting about practicing rational emotive behavior therapy (REBT) is how a sizable number of my clients, via a simple realignment of their thinking (for instance, minimizing the words "have to" and/or "awful" in their vocabulary) are able to quickly take an abundant amount of pressure off themselves and their relationships with others. One or two simple but powerful ideas can have a heavy positive impact on your emotions; on the other hand, you can be exposed to a smorgasbord of ideas over a long period of time and make negligible progress in emotional self-control. Short-term self-help, with emphasis on rapidly learning specific ideas that contribute to increasing life's enjoyments, had best not be ruled out. Furthermore, not only can you learn to help yourself in shorter periods of time with simple ideas with a high level of emotional self-control, but you can also use these same leanings to maintain gains for longer periods of time!

The advantages to thinking in such short-term problem-solving possibilities include:

1. *Sparking of a more immediate sense of anticipation and participation in helping of self.* The shorter the expectation of length of change, the more eagerness in moving toward that change is likely to be generated. The closer you picture yourself to reaching your goal, the keener and more decided your energy level is likely to be.

2. *Encourages better organization of resources and more efficient use of time.* The longer the time period given to complete a project, the greater the temptation and likeli-

hood to procrastinate. Having shorter deadline expectations is an encouragement to muster the energy to put your abilities to good use sooner rather than later, now rather than never.

3. *Promotes self-reliance.* Limitations of time prompt more dependence on self in personal problem-solving efforts. It takes time to recruit others on your behalf, and the less time you give yourself to gather your resources, the more self-initiative you will likely take.

4. *Conveys anticipatory success.* Thinking in terms of short-run personal gains encourages success confidence. This anticipatory view implies that such goals are reachable in a short period of time or else you wouldn't have self-suggested the short-term ideal to begin with. In other words, you can use the self-fulfilling promise to slant the odds for success in your favor. If you look for something, you are more likely to find it. Whether you look for forever-and-a-day change possibilities or whether you seek shorter change possibilities, you are likely to find them.

5. *Is a vote for performance confidence.* Promoting the idea that you believe you are not an emotional cripple and can therefore consider the possibility of turning your life around in spritely fashion is a shot in the arm for increased confidence.

After you have considered the reasonable possibility that short-term self help is in your ballpark, review the following characteristics of a time-limited game plan to helping yourself.

1. *Does a lot of one thing rather than a little bit of a lot of things.* Be specific! Zero in on precise thoughts, feelings, and behaviors that you wish to change. Short-term problem solving is as nondirective as good surgery. Concentrating on a specific area of change funnels your energies rather than diluting them. Consequently, you

will be less likely to hold back effort and as a result will strongly apply rather than weakly gloss over collective plans.

2. *Appreciate and apply the domino theory of problem solving.* Success tends to breed success, once you establish it. Therefore, you don't have to solve all your problems, but if you learn principles that will help you to cope with most of them, you can apply those principles as a way of preventing or correcting future problems. Whether heading problems off at the pass or correcting them as they occur, wise, successful, problem-solving principles prepare you to deal with practically all of your concerns. This is one of the exciting features of rational emotive behavior therapy: Once you establish success with its problem-solving model, you can continue to more automatically use its ideas any time in the future.

3. *Take on a no-nonsense outlook.*   Don't drag your feet waiting for time to "heal."   Instead, promptly get down to brass tacks and take action on behalf of yourself.

4. *Look for fast-acting models.*   Think of others you have known who seemed to make prompt, forced turnarounds in their life.   Seek from them the secret of their success and apply those learnings in your own life.

5. *Spend minimal time examining the past.* The past doesn't get any better.   One of the best remedies for past failures is success experiences in the present.   As you figure out how not to disadvantage yourself in the present, you will learn what you did wrong in the past.   Giving the past preferential treatment will only needlessly mark time.

6. *Don't pretend to not know what you do know.*   Try to build from your strengths, what you can do and have done to help yourself, rather than what you have been unable to do and haven't done.   Examine closely those times in your life that you have successfully coped with adversity, what you did right, and how you can apply such abilities now and in the future.

7. *Encourage yourself by discouragement.* Don't fool yourself. If you have decided to not put forth the necessary effort to complete a project, be honest enough with yourself to admit it. Don't put yourself down for your decision to defer solving a particular problem. Instead, pick up the beat by using that energy to solve those problems that you presently want to work against. Discourage yourself from wasting time tiptoeing around what you presently aren't willing to do, and encourage yourself to reinvest your resources in what you are now willing to do.

8. *Go for the light rather than the darkness.* Work against your problems as you see them, not as you think you might not be seeing them or by how others are seeing them. Trust yourself to identify what your problems are. Try not to second-guess yourself or let others do so as this will likely result in weakly touching down on a variety of problems without strongly coming down on any one of them.

9. *Evaluate yourself for problems that you don't have.* Double check to be sure that you're not making yourself afraid of your own emotional shadow. Perhaps instead of being depressed you may merely feel sad; instead of guilt, regret; in place of anger, displeasure; and instead of fear, apprehension. Sadness, regret, displeasure, and apprehension are not emotionally disturbed states to begin with; to mislabel them as depression, guilt, anger, or fear, which are emotional disturbances, will lengthen your problem-solving efforts.

10. *Consider the solution as problem possibility.* Rather than overemphasize change, consider the idea that as a remarkably imperfect human being you might be doing yourself a huge favor by accepting the alternative solution of learning to coexist with your shortcoming. The sky is *not* the limit for overcoming personal deficiencies; work hard at changing your flaws when possible, but keep a

decent respect for human limitations, including your own limitations in overcoming personal problems.

11. *Accept the idea that you affect yourself more than you're affected.* I believe it was George Bernard Shaw who said, "Things don't happen to me, I happen to them." Taking such a view of fuller responsibility for self avoids wasting a lot of time changing others and circumstances that are likely not to budge. Individuals change quicker than systems and can rise above them. For instance, if you find dissatisfactions in your family system, change your response to it rather than trying to change it.

12. *Avoid comfort traps.* If you wait until you're comfortable before you initiate problem-solving efforts, you may end up waiting at least half a lifetime. Instead, take your fears with you until you better acclimate yourself to them.

13. *Avoid bottomless pits.* Ideas that indicate you "need" what you want, or that you have to prove your worth, will send you on a wild problem-solving goose chase. It takes a long time to find something that doesn't exist. Need-seeking and self-esteem-building tactics are never-ending in their desperate search for things whose existence cannot be proven: that humans have needs or requirements and that humans have worth generally, that some humans are more worthwhile than others, or that a given individual is more worthy or esteemed at one point in time than at another.

14. *Exclude vagueness.* Unspecified goals (e.g., "I want to find out who I am," "I want to get myself squared away," "I want to find out what I'm about," "I want to get my head on straight") had best be tracked down to specific circumstances and projects. Substituting such ambiguous goals with a list of "things that I want to do, touch, taste, feel, smell, or otherwise experience in the time that I have left in the rest of my life" allows you to hang your hat on more concrete and lifelike, as opposed to mystical, objectives.

Following is a list of those thoughts and attitudes that discourage the possibility of quicker change as well as countering self-talk that supports the idea of moving on sooner rather than later down your problem-solving road.

IDEAS THAT HAMPER SHORT-TERM PROBLEM SOLVING	COUNTERING IDEAS THAT CONTRIBUTE TO SHORT-TERM PROBLEM SOLVING
"But I've been this way all my life."	"If I ate manure all my life, I wouldn't have to continue to eat it."
"My parents and grandparents were the same way."	"I am not a clone of my blood relatives and can set myself apart from them."
"I come from a long line of character problems."	"I can shorten the long line of character problems I come from by not getting in line."
"Most people, given my circumstances, would handle it the same way."	"I'm not most people - I'm me."
"It's so much easier to do things the way I always have."	"It's harder, in the long run, to continue in my self-defeating ways."
"You can't teach an old dog new tricks."	"An old human can teach himself or herself new tricks."
"Rome wasn't built in a day."	"Rebuilding myself is something I have more control over than the building of a city."
"I'm too set in my ways."	"Nothing is carved in granite."
"It took me forever and a day to become so well practiced, it will take me at least as equally long to undo my habits."	"What am I asking myself to do that hasn't been done before? Don't exaggerate your problems and don't overestimate the time needed for correcting them."
"I can't change any faster than the time it took me to get this way."	"If I take the right shortcuts, the return trip home can be much shorter than the original destination."

IDEAS THAT HAMPER SHORT-TERM PROBLEM SOLVING *(Cont'd)*	COUNTERING IDEAS THAT CONTRIBUTE TO SHORT-TERM PROBLEM SOLVING *(Cont'd)*
"My problems have been a slow train coming, and correcting them will naturally be like a slow train going."	"I may not be able to determine the speed of trains, but I can determine the speed of my recovery."
"After all these years, it's so natural to be this way, and to act unnaturally seems like a long way off."	"With practice, what seems unnatural can be made to seem natural, and with neglect, what I have made to seem natural can be made to seem unnatural."
"Go slow; others might not like it if I change too fast."	"True, others might not like it if I change too quickly, but others might also think that I'm not changing quickly enough. I'd best put others' disapproval or approval aside and concentrate more on what I really want."

With long-term expectations as your friend, who needs enemies? Use the expectation factor in your favor and work it for you by giving your problem-solving abilities credit for the possibility of rapid personal change. When you allow yourself to try something different and find it helpful for the purposes of more effective living, you will likely make yourself inclined to continue giving yourself such an advantage. Giving yourself the benefit of such basis for comparison can be done in a short period of time. If you allow yourself to take on a more adventuresome, experimenting approach to life, and force yourself to do so whether you feel like it or not, solving your longstanding problems in short periods of time can be made to be well within your grasp. Don't expect miracles from short-term personal problem solving (in fact don't expect miracles from anything), but expect results. There is no automatic connection between the length of existence of the problem and the time it will take to better cope with it. Be open for quick getaway possibilities; don't lock yourself into such a fatalistic equation or you may lock your-self out of more prompt self-help possibilities.

There's the story of the person who went to an analyst for a mental status assessment. After his evaluation, the therapist said to the client, "Brother, do you have problems; it's going to take me 7 years of psychotherapy with you three times a week to solve them." The patient replied, "Well Doc, that takes care of your problems, now how about mine?" In taking care of your own problems, keep in mind that maybe there is no such thing as a quick fix, but maybe there is a quicker one. Speed it up; you can always slow down. Assume yourself to be capable of quicker change than the length of your problem may reflect. That way, you will likely get more problem-solving mileage more often - in shorter periods of time. Go for the short rather than the long of self-help. By expecting more timely results in shorter periods of time, you may well take yourself beyond what the original self-fulfilling promise would lead you to expect.

Note. From *Feeling Right When Things Go Wrong* by Bill Borcherdt. Copyright © 1998, Professional Resource Exchange, Inc., P.O. Box 15560, Sarasota, FL 34277-1560.

Is "One Day at a Time" Really the One Way To Live the One Life That You Will Ever Have?

Rational emotive behavior therapy (REBT) is known for spoiling the party of many of conventional wisdom's well-known, trite-sounding clichés. The motto that supports the absolute necessity of living "one day at a time" is no exception. Slogans that "sound good" and "feel good" often do not hold water when reality tested and are therefore not good for you. Living "one day at a time," as popularized by Alcoholics Anonymous and often unthinkingly adopted with much fever and fervor by other problem-solving strategies, has many drawbacks that often go unnoticed. It's as if the frenzied, zealous manner in which this simplistic idea is embraced blocks a broader, potentially better view that questions and counters its false assumption - that one size fits all and therefore it should, must, ought to be worn - or you can expect to falter. REBT is antibigotry and takes aim at such all-or-nothing falsehoods.

This guide will identify the loopholes in this focus-on-today-only philosophy of living so that one then has a basis for comparison prior to deciding on, renewing, or discarding this living-in-the-immediate principle. Education about an idea rather than blind faith in a principle will usually result in a better informed decision that will likely better contribute to one's short- and long-range best interests. Drawbacks of "one day at a time" include:

1. *Daily defines and renews life as a struggle.* Life can be more than simply plodding along. This attitude sets limits on the human potential to enjoy life more fully. REBT tries to get you past your original emotional disturbance, such as anger, fear, guilt, or depression. It then helps you to make yourself less disturbable in the future. Lastly, it encourages you to develop or actualize yourself in ways that *you* choose; to have more of a ball in life! "One day at a time" applications may help you through the first effort, but will likely hinder the last two possibilities.
2. *Implies and is often accompanied by sacredness.* This limited vision is often put forth as "the way" to live. Such an ultimate perspective fails to mention that the happiest of people often have a long-range view of living.
3. *Narrowed application possibilities.* Short-term thinking may be good for some people, some of the time, for instance, in getting through a crisis. To boldly posit that it is a "must" for all or even most is to imply that humans are clones of one another.
4. *Encourages a dependency on recovery.* To forcefully cling to a mode of thinking that may assist you through a crisis will leave you with excessive emotional baggage once you have weathered the immediate storm. How many times during the days, months, and years of your life are you going to compulsively make yourself fight the battle before you realize that the war has already been won?
5. *Discounts the dreams and schemes of the future as servicing your mental health.* One thing we know for sure about the future - it's where we are going to spend the rest of our lives. Why not capitalize on the juice and zest that comes from aspiring hope for down-the-road plans,

projects, and ambitions? Vital absorption in these types of future hopes often not only helps to make your world go around, but also keeps you from getting yourself dizzy and tizzy! One-day-at-a-time notions discourage thinking in terms of eventual vital possibilities.

6. *Fosters burdensomeness and drudgery, discourages play-fulness.* All work and toil with little play makes for a dull existence rather than for sharper living. Keenness to life's joys is watered down because a one-day-at-a-time view presents life as a serious grind to be tended to daily in this intent manner. Too much work in the game of life blocks a more decided sense of joy that one may be capable of experiencing.

7. *Doesn't extend success.* Present successes can be stretched to the benefit of your future if they are carried forth beyond today. Projecting present successes into the future by self-stating today your intention to use their methods tomorrow is discouraged by a today-and-today-only stance.

8. *Ignores individual differences.* The fact that an individual or group of individuals finds it convenient to buy into the popular buzz words of "one day at a time" is a far cry from proving that one size fits all. Yet those who religiously abide by this outlook seem to lose focus on that simple reality in the zeal of their support for this philosophy. Heaven forbid if a member of the support group would dare to think any differently! Such an individualized perspective would likely be admonished and its holder treated as an outcast. Insistencies that round pegs be put into square holes are attempts to override free will and freer thinking.

9. *Projects a misery-likes-company mentality.* "By God, if my life is so painful that I find it necessary to not look ahead, then you too must define your lot in life in similar negative terms, and how dare you betray my miserable view of life. If I can't be happy unless I take it one day

at a time, then you must not either." This is the hidden agenda of the true believer who demands that you live your life in the present.

10. *Discourages seeking and seeing a light at the end of the tunnel.* Finding a light at the end of a tunnel and seeing that there doesn't have to be a train coming at you can only be done by looking ahead, oftentimes well beyond today.

11. *Encourages seat-of-the-pants, fly-by-night rather than planned action problem solving.* If you don't know where you're going, you may never get there. To realize where that destination might be requires a road map that will take you well beyond today. A more limited view may serve as a Band-Aid that allows you to feel better today, but it will likely restrict you from doing major surgery in getting on with and getting better for the rest of your life.

12. *Discourages potential membership.* Those in the recovery process of putting their lives together may find the group's steadfast, rigid, golden rule of one day at a time, and the fanaticism and narrow-mindedness often attached to it, to be distasteful enough to boycott.

There you have it! Twelve good reasons to approach this sacred cow of an ideal with all its tarnish in a questioning rather than an unquestioning manner. Reconsideration of any dogma can do practically nothing but good. To observe more objectively the light of day can prove to be quite enlightening. This is not to say that a "one-day-at-a-time" viewpoint is never in order. *Once* in a while it is *one* way to live in the *one* life you will ever have.

Know-It-Alls:
Knowing, Understanding,
Accepting, and
Coping With Them

"I can't get a word in edgewise. He always thinks he knows everything." This familiar complaint is about people who like to appear that they possess infinite wisdom about everything from soup to nuts - except why they require themselves to act in such all-knowing ways. This guide will fill in this knowledge gap of the know-it-alls and better equip you to deal with them, including how *you* can get a word in edgewise by interrupting them without intruding on them.

Know-it-alls pose both an inner and an outer challenge. Inwardly, use your association with them to work on raising your tolerance and not your temperature level by making it a point to upset yourself less about their talent to dominate a conversation. Outwardly, learn some crisp verbal and nonverbal assertion skills to get your foot in the door so that you can express yourself. Preferably work on the inner problem first, as this is where you can control more of the variables. Because know-it-alls are well practiced, management of their attitudes, such as "I long ago discovered the truth and I know that you can't wait to hear what it is," and "Everybody is entitled to my opinion," will be no easy task. What is required is a combination of knowledge and protective action as described in the following suggestions.

1. *Learn your ABCs* (of emotional self-control). Don't trip your own trigger. As much as you may tempt yourself to fight fire with fire, learn to dim rather than ignite the flames of your frustrations when associating with the all-knowing person. Angry, aggressive, and hostile tactics, where you barge in and take on the other's godlike manner, will only duplicate the problem. To prevent your own overreaction, apply rational emotive behavior therapy's theory of emotional containments as created by Dr. Ellis.

   A (Activating event, something happens.) Someone is quick to jump in and begins to tell you all he or she knows, including all he or she thinks that you don't know about a given subject.

   B (Belief system, what thoughts you give to yourself about the other's supposed ingenious comments.)

   - "He has no right to flaunt his claimed knowledge about this topic."
   - "It's terrible to be exposed to her verbal diarrhea."
   - "I can't stand the way he is running off at the mouth."
   - "I have to get her to stop exercising her jaws the way she is."
   - "What a fool he is making me out to be by treating me so foolishly."
   - "What an ass she is for acting asininely."
   - "I'll fix his wagon for only bringing me along for the ride and not letting me say my piece."

   C (Emotional consequences, feelings you created from your thoughts at "B".) Anger, rage, anguish, fury, or vindictiveness.

   D (Debate, dispute, different ways of thinking that you develop as a result of challenging your original ideas at "B".)

- "Where is the scientific evidence that this self-proclaimed wise person cannot flaunt what she believes to be all the knowledge in the world for all the world to hear, including me?"
- "Granted, he gives himself the runs with his verbal diarrhea, but is it really terrible, like I make it out to be?"
- "I can take her alleged pearls of wisdom either standing up or sitting down, and, although I find her unsolicited comments annoying, they for sure are standable or sitable."
- "Although I would like to find a way to unlock the secret to getting him to keep his big yapper shut, it is not the absolute necessity that I complainingly make it out to be."
- "She certainly is treating me foolishly by trying to snow me under with her verbal bombardments, but in no way does her behavior represent me as being a fool!"
- "Likewise, though his asinine behavior is a pain in the ass, in no way does this represent him as being an ass."
- "Do I want to feel better now by giving her both the angry and vindictive barrels, or do I want to feel *and* get better for the rest of my life by increasing my tolerance, forgiveness, and undamning acceptance of this not-so-perfect person?"

E (New effects - more flexible, tolerant beliefs about life generally and about negative-acting people specifically.) For example: "Others have a right to be wrong, and it's not terrible when they freely choose to be so." Creation of feelings that are in your better interest, such as irritation, displeasure, and annoyance. Production of behaviors that better attend to your self-interest, such as doing away with varying forms of counteraggression and punishment, yet acting in a firm and no-nonsense way to bring attention to your displeasure.

Following the rational emotive behavior therapy model allows you to understand and experience the fact that you can affect yourself less by others' contrary behavior while at the same time protecting yourself from it.

2. *Don't presume change.*   Cutting down on your inner upset will increase the chances that some of the practical advice to follow will help. However, don't assume that changing your inner and/or outer response will result in your associate turning over a new, less-obnoxious-acting leaf. Instead, understand that he or she is well practiced in the art of boastful knowledge, and push yourself to accept him or her in spite of the obvious flaw. That way, you can assure change within yourself in the direction of a more tolerant thinking and behaving you. Then:

3. *Attribute his or her conduct.* Reflect on the telltale signs that reveal the other's insecurities. Know-it-alls often secretly believe that they know nothing and are nothing. They desperately will attempt to make up for this inner hurt by believing they are somebody as long as others think they know something. Then:

4. *Self-state empathy.* Vigorously tell yourself ideas that reflect active understanding and acceptance of the other's insecurity handicap, for example:

- "Isn't it unfortunate that my associate makes himself feel so meager that he can come up with nothing better to do than try to diminish me by putting himself up on a pedestal of self-proclaimed knowledge."
- "I can sense that my associate is hurting by the way she expounds seeming wisdom about practically every topic under the sun. Let me see how I can do myself

a favor by not getting myself caught up in her proclamation."
- "Best I treat my sidekick with heavy doses of compassion to lighten both our loads of frustration."

5. *Use humor.* Blend in with the flow of the verbal attack
rather than meet it head on. Don't take others as seriously as they are taking themselves.

6. *Separate out "associated with" from "dependent upon."*
You may rub elbows with those who think they know
more than they probably do, but this does not mean that
you are required to make yourself dependent upon those
people being any different than they naturally are. A
common mistake of codependent reasoning is that association with a disturbed person by necessity has to lead to
you becoming disturbed yourself.

7. *Interrupt without intruding.* Draw attention to yourself
by assertively signaling to the other that you wish to get
your two cents of position statement in. Examples of
efforts geared toward making communication a two-way
street, where it is made convenient for others to respond
to you rather than you simply responding to them, are:

- *Persistently state, "let me interrupt" and then do so.*
Assert yourself by directly signaling that you wish to
be heard and then tactfully present your position.

- *Use restatement procedures.* Knifing into the conversation with "Let me see if I understood what you just
said" and then doing a brief retake of what you
thought your ears just heard can interrupt the ongoing
chatter of the know-it-all.

- *Summarization tactics.* Active-directively offering a
complete review of the sender's message, and not
letting up until you are done, can derail the motor-
mouthed-acting person.

- *Sharp flattery.* Blatantly interjecting "I admire the strength of your convictions" (without necessarily agreeing with them) has the potential for taking the wind out of the sails of the hot-aired, yapping individual.
- *Acknowledge effort.* Repeated reflection of "I can see you have given this matter a lot of thought" may appeal to his or her sense of humility long enough to take the hot air out of his or her lead balloon of unsolicited teaching.
- *Get below the surface.* Get past the content of his or her message and actively attend to the know-it-all's feelings behind his or her message. People rarely believe they are understood at the feeling level. When they are, they often stop themselves in their tracks long enough to reflect on your end of the conversation.
- *Openly express disappointment about exclusion.* Simply stating that you don't appreciate the neglect of your input and that you, too, have some important things to be said and heard can impress upon the other the advisability of hearing you out.
- *Signal inaccessibility.* Turning away, focusing attention on your watch, stretching, and yawning are all ways to cue the other to your disinterest in being used as an indefinite sounding board.
- *Use of hand signals.* Literally signaling for a time out, motioning the other to stop by holding up your hands palms up, and mimicking turning a key in front of your mouth are all silent ways of disarming conversation dominance.
- *Expression of nonverbal concerns.* Raising your eyebrows to reflect disapproval or using facial expressions that indicate confusion can assist in neutralizing the other's running off at the mouth.

When used in combination, inner and outer methods for protection and making contact can help in meeting and beating the challenges of the boastful-talking person. Don't get yourself down about the other's uppityness. Understand another's holier-than-thou agenda as an effort to disguise feelings of unworthier-than-all. Don't play psychological one-downmanship with yourself in responding to another's psychological one-upmanship. The know-it-all's motto is, "I have to be perfectly achieving in possessing and expressing superior knowledge to all people, all of the time, or else I'm perfectly inferior." Understanding know-it-alls' self-judgment handicap, while accepting them in spite of it, provides you with the know-how for more clearheadedly coping with them.

Note. From *Feeling Right When Things Go Wrong* by Bill Borcherdt. Copyright © 1998, Professional Resource Exchange, Inc., P.O. Box 15560, Sarasota, FL 34277-1560.

Jump Out of Your Skin
And Get It Over With:
Accepting the Worst
To Get to the Better

Rational emotive behavior therapy (REBT) contends that solutions vary in their usefulness; that with some types of remedies, the solution can be made into the problem! Putting yourself through an emotional wringer may not appear to be the rational thing to do, but REBT's preference for elegant, high-level solutions shows how more comprehensive, comfortable emotional rustproofing can be gained by exposure to the highest level of discomfort. Let me explain how this theory of putting yourself through hell and back works.

Accepting the worst that could happen prevents worrying about it actually happening. By vigorously telling yourself "If I fail I fail, tough but not terrible" or "If I feel uncomfortable, then I do; that would be annoying but tolerable," you will make yourself less inclined to stew about these negative possibilities happening. On the other hand, by putting success and/or comfort on a pedestal by convincing yourself that "I must, under all conditions and at all times, succeed" or "No matter what my situation, I must always feel comfort in being there, as not being given this ideal would be too much of an extraordinary event to bear," you will startle yourself about such negative events whether they occur or not! True, you may be able to control for success or comfort and feel good about having done so. But what is more likely to happen is that you will end up putting undue pressure on yourself to gain the solution, only to create additional stress-pocket problems that will block success. Even if by chance you gain the love and job of your life you will be looking over your shoulder thinking, "Yes, I feel better from success and with comfort, but what if the next time I'm not so lucky? Wouldn't that be awful and horrible?" Going into the mouth of the dragon accepting and tolerantly entertaining the possibility of failure and/or discomfort leaves you looking straight ahead, concentrating on your goals rather than seeing shadows behind you.

One excellent method of applying the elegant solution is by rehearsing coming to grips with the worst that could occur. Developing more emotional immunity to that possibility is REBT's version of rational-emotive imagery. This emotional conditioning strategy goes like this:

- Close your eyes and vividly picture what you're most worrying yourself about actually happening (e.g., being harshly criticized, making a public blunder, losing out in love, or feeling anxious or panicky).
- Meet this worry on *your terms*. Go to it rather than holding back waiting for its possibilities to come to you. Do this by making yourself feel highly disturbed - that is, guilty, depressed, angry, or fearful - about these negative matters. Force yourself to give yourself a knot in your stomach about the worst possible outcome that could occur. Don't hold back; make contact in your thoughts and in your feelings with the worst of the worst.
- Then, in the next breath, substitute a different emotion - not to try unrealistically to make yourself emotionless but, rather to experience a lessened, different emotion. Use your creativity of mind to replace your emotional disturbance with emotional disappointment, sadness, concern, or regret. Keenly and decidedly acknowledge these more moderate feeling states but don't throw gasoline on them.

- Practice doesn't make perfect, but it can help. Practice this exercise designed to help you to better help yourself control your emotions, once or twice a day for 30 days, and see if you don't start to put yourself well on the road to jumping in and out of your skin in the service of your long-range emotional well-being.

In an effort to further make my point about the elegant solution being a more complete solution, I will first identify a list of limited, inelegant "positive thoughts" that will help you to feel better because they comfort you with the possibility of success in making things right. Then, I will illustrate rational thoughts that will help you not only to feel better but also to elegantly and more completely get better, because they (a) help to clear your head so as to increase the chances of making things right, and (b) point to how to get yourself less upset in the event that things are made to go wrong.

POSITIVE THOUGHTS THAT ASSIST IN TEMPORARILY FEELING BETTER	RATIONAL THOUGHTS THAT HELP TO MORE PERMANENTLY GET BETTER
"I know I can succeed and I know I will."	"I think I can succeed but won't know for sure until I do."
"Everything will work out for the better."	"Everything could and hopefully will work out for the better."
"I just sense that it's going to be OK."	"I have a sense that it's likely to turn out OK."
"My higher power will watch out for me and see that all things will come together."	"My guardian angel may well be on strike (again), so I'd best monitor bringing more things together."
"It's no big deal if it doesn't work out. Really, what's the difference?"	"It is a big deal if things don't work out - just not bigger than life."

POSITIVE THOUGHTS THAT ASSIST IN TEMPORARILY FEELING BETTER *(Cont'd)*	RATIONAL THOUGHTS THAT HELP TO MORE PERMANENTLY GET BETTER *(Cont'd)*
"I've succeeded before and I know I will again."	"I have succeeded before, but I have also failed before. The fact that I've succeeded before doesn't necessarily mean I am going to succeed again."
"Because I've practiced so much, I know I can and will succeed."	"Practice can be helpful but doesn't guarantee success."
"I can't imagine myself failing."	"I'm human; humans fail. I can imagine myself failing, though I hope not to."
"I've done all the right things, so matters have to turn out for the best."	"Because I've done many of the right things, I am optimistic about my possibilities to succeed."
"Anyone who tries as hard as I do is bound to succeed."	"Anyone who tries as hard as I do is more likely to succeed."
"Think positive, because positive thinking is the answer to everything."	"Positive thinking is not the key to the universe; furthermore, I'm not sure what is."

Positive thoughts can sometimes be helpful in a limited way. Rational thoughts, because they plant seeds of tolerance and acceptance, which are key ingredients of mental health, are more likely to help you to grow into a more well-rounded human being who is better prepared for action. Positive thoughts temporarily pacify fears; rational thoughts overcome these same frights. Positive thoughts provide immediate comfort; rational thoughts help you to feel better for the rest of your life. Positive thoughts encourage dependent personality tendencies; rational thoughts overhaul dependent tendencies while encouraging interdependent and independent strivings.

So, go ahead and jump out of your emotional skin. Meet the worst of your worst fears on your turf and terms. See if this home-court advantage will help you to win out over your overreactions. Look before and after you leap and see if you don't discover how this more flexible strategy, in which you leave a margin for even the worst error, allows you to better service your emotional well-being.

Note. From *Feeling Right When Things Go Wrong* by Bill Borcherdt. Copyright © 1998, Professional Resource Exchange, Inc., P.O. Box 15560, Sarasota, FL 34277-1560.

Mirror, Mirror on the Wall -
Who Is the Fairest
Of Them All?
Compassion, Not Comparison

Humans are the only animals that observe themselves, then draw conclusions in the form of inferences and ideas about what they see. More often than not, these notions are faulty and irrational. Seldom are these assumptions reviewed for their accuracy and contributions to emotional health. This spectator tendency, which has individuals spying on themselves, often is done via distorted thinking seen in (a) exaggerated conclusions taken on about one's performances, relationships with others, abilities, or disabilities, and (b) the self-judgment rating game in which people give themselves a good mark for their advantages and a bad one for their disadvantages. Examples of typical assumptions are:

- "I didn't do as good a job as my partner."
- "The boss didn't say hi to me today - he is probably going to fire me."
- "My mate purposefully didn't show up for our date."
- "I'm not as intelligent as my brother."
- "I didn't get as many Valentine's Day cards as my roommate."
- "I'm not as popular as my sister."
- "I'm not as close to my parents as my brothers and sisters are."

- "I have more body fat than my girlfriend."
- "I'm not as creative as the rest of the family."
- "I'm not as sexy as most men (women)."
- "I'm not as well known or popular as other psycho-therapists in the community."
- "I probably won't get nominated for teacher of the year in my district."
- "My IQ isn't as high as most people's."
- "I have less education than anyone on this planning committee."
- "I was intentionally not invited to the party (even though I didn't want to go to begin with)."
- "I'm sure I won't be getting the raise or promotion that I had hoped for at the end of the year."
- "I didn't spend enough time with my children when they were young."
- "I didn't make the right decision in getting married."
- "I'm the worst in my class in spelling."
- "I have the most peculiarly shaped body of anyone in my gym class."
- "I never have and never will win a trophy for any-thing."
- "The financial investments I have made were foolish."
- "I gave the worst speech in the class."
- "I say the stupidest things."
- "I always feel uncomfortable in social situations, un-like others who are always calm and relaxed."

From all walks of life, people observe their activities and create vultures: negative inferences about what they see. Such inferences may be right or wrong. If distorted, as they oftentimes are, they will prey on and sap emotional strength in their own right. However, by themselves, crooked observances will not cause emotional disturbances, such as anger, depression, guilt, or anxiety. Crooked thinking will. Irrational beliefs about your personal viewing are at the core of your upsets. Let me give some common illustrations:

INFERENCE (What you believe to be true)	IRRATIONAL BELIEFS (Demanding, overreactive, exaggerated, personalized ideas about what your observation and inferences mean for you)
"I'm not as close to my parents as my brothers and sisters."	"How terrible that I am not as close to my parents as I should be. What an utterly rotten person I am due to such distance."
"I'm not as sexy as most men (women)."	"Sexiness is next to godliness and because I'm not as sexy as the rest I must be the devil. I am my sex appeal and if it is bad, I'm bad."
"I was intentionally not invited to the party (even though I didn't want to go to begin with)."	"What's wrong with me that others purposefully selected against me? I can't stand such rebuke (even though I didn't want to go to begin with)."
"I'm not keeping up with the Joneses."	"I have to keep pace with others' material advantages, and when I don't I have to deem myself inferior due to my inferior socioeconomic standing."
"I'm not as well-known or popular as other psychotherapists in the community."	"I absolutely have to be king/queen of the hill as to psychotherapeutic notoriety, and because second fiddle means second class, I simply cannot bear such a runner-up standing."
"I say the stupidest things."	"I should only make intelligent statements, and it's awful and I'm awfully stupid when I don't."
"I always feel uncomfortable in social situations, unlike others who are calm and relaxed."	"I have to feel comfortable around others, and I can't tolerate it or myself when I'm not."

In all these examples, what you suspect to be true by way of self-stated inferences will create moderate disappointment. Dissatisfactions are made to be amplified into the emotional

intensity that characterizes disturbance via irrational philosophies. These can be replaced by more tolerant, accepting ideas
such as:

- "True, I didn't do as good a job as my partner and as
  a result did not get the promotion that he did. False,
  that I'm a bad person for not achieving my ambition."
- "Correct that my boss didn't say hi to me. Correct
  that it's possible he may have a bead on firing me.
  Correct that this would disadvantage me. Incorrect
  that even if I never found another job, my life would
  come to an end or I could not still achieve some
  degree of happiness."
- "It may be accurate that my mate intentionally didn't
  meet me when she said she would - but does she not
  have the right to purposefully inconvenience me?"
- "I may possess inferior intelligence than my brother,
  but it would be foolish to judge myself by this one
  trait, several traits, or to put it more purely - for anything."
- "The fact that I didn't get as many Valentine's Day
  cards as my roommate does not reflect negatively on
  me."
- "Just as sure as I'm not as popular as my sis-
  ter/brother, so too I'm not less of a person because of
  that."
- "I'm not as close to my parents as my brother and
  sister, but that doesn't mean there is a universal law
  that says I have to be."
- "My excess body fat is not good, but it doesn't represent my value to myself."
- "Creativity tends to run in families, but the fact that I
  didn't inherit that trait like others in my family doesn't
  mean I have to get down on myself about it."
- "I don't have to give myself ego problems for not
  being among the very sexy."

- "I do my work as a psychotherapist, but I am not my work and I don't have to make such a to-do about not being as favored as I would like to be."
- "Not being nominated for teacher of the year in my district is regretful but not catastrophic or demeaning."
- "The fact that my IQ isn't as high as most people doesn't mean I have to go through life with my head between my legs."
- "My not getting invited to the party reflects others' oversights, tastes, or preferences, it does not reflect on or discredit me."
- "It is regretful that I didn't spend as much time with my children as I wish I had when they were young, but that's all it is; it's not terrible, all-important, or sacred."
- "Making the wrong decision about marrying or anything else isn't bigger than life or the most hideous of all possible crimes."
- "Granted, I ranked the worst in my class in spelling, but that doesn't make me a worse person."
- "My having a peculiarly shaped body is not shameful or qualify me for wormhood."
- "Winning or losing a trophy does not make me a winner or loser, but a person who wins or loses."
- "The fact that I have made some foolish financial investments does not make me a fool. If it did, how could a fool learn from his or her mistakes?"
- "Giving the worst speech in class was disappointing but not a disaster."
- "Sometimes I do put my foot in my mouth, but I'm human and humans apparently do this type of thing - so such actions do not make me subhuman."
- "Foolishly making myself uncomfortable in social situations does not mean that such self-imposed discomfort is not bearable or that I am required to put myself down for such foolishness."

Preferential rational emotive behavior therapy (REBT) corrects irrational beliefs about inferences *before* checking for possible misunderstanding about these observations. This is called the elegant solution in problem solving in that even if the worst original assumption turns out to be true, it can be tolerantly and self-acceptingly coped with.

When reach exceeds grasp, negative comparisons followed by critical self-evaluations are often put to not so good use. Human limits can be better served by putting such hasty over-generalizations to rest. Such comparative, extended views about leading an imperfect existence in an imperfect world had best be replaced with a more compassionate stance. Instead of trying to prove who is the fairest of them all, be more than fairly compassionate with yourself in an effort to reflect greater emotional well-being.

Owning Up to
The Facts of Self-Pity

"Let the baby have his milk" - because he will likely whine and scream to the high heavens if he doesn't get it. "Don't cry over spilled milk" is a slogan that encourages the person who loses an advantage to do something about trying to get a similar advantage someplace else, rather than childishly stewing about the going without in the present. Because maturity is often viewed as putting away childish antics, few are willing to admit they are acting like a crybaby when they sulk about not getting their own way. This tendency to deny childish fault makes self-pity perhaps the most difficult emotion to responsibly own up to. Yet, until such "woe is me" tendencies are admitted, this special form of self-indulgence will linger, free to wear thin your personal and interpersonal happiness.

Self-pity puts a strain and is a drain on your emotional well-being. Getting yourself past its handicaps requires a mix of removing the self-imposed barriers that prevent recognizing and admitting its existence, identifying its often-present trademarks that cause it to stand by itself as a form of self-centeredness, and undoing its mechanical structure by replacing its irrational foundation with more sensible ways of viewing life and people in it who do not fit your specifications.

The following self-statements are dead giveaways that you have allowed self-pity to raise its ugly head. Recognize them as such so that you may begin to undo their foothold in your mind.

Tip-offs to self-pity:

- "Poor me."
- "Why me?"
- "Not me again."
- "I always get the shaft."
- "Things never work out for me."
- "Every time I put my best foot forward I get it stepped on."
- "I'm always in the wrong place at the wrong time."
- "I never get any breaks."
- "It's always my fault."
- "For once I would like life to be fair."
- "I always get the short end of the stick."
- "I deserve better."
- "This is not fair to me."
- "Give me a break!"
- "All I ask for is half a chance."
- "What ever happened to justice?"
- "Fair my foot!"
- "Just once I'd like to be first."
- "All I ask for is a little bit more of what I'm getting."
- "Is it asking too much to be given a fair deal?"
- "For crying out loud, foiled and unfairly treated again!"
- "What did I ever do to deserve this?"
- "What kind of raw deal did I get now?"
- "Just one time I'd like a piece of the action too!"
- "Never has a person tried so hard in return for so little."
- "The least life can do is to let me sneak ahead once in a while."
- "No way do I ever get my own way!"
- "I am owed the things in life that I miss!"
- "Because I seldom ask for anything and when I do I don't ask for much, I should at least get what I want once in a while."

Cry me a river, will you! These hard-on-yourself ideas that reek with intolerance and demands will give you a bad case of the pities. They are rooted in a faulty philosophy of deservingness compiled in these central irrational beliefs:

- "I'm not getting my own way as I deservedly must."
- "The world and people in it have to be fair and always give me what would be to my advantage."
- "When the world and people in it don't strike my fancy in a way that I can strike it rich, I'll whine and bemoan my plight so as to (a) get even with these adverse universal factors, even if it means throwing the baby out with the bathwater, and (b) magically change these factors that are against me and get those who select against me to change their bias. After all, if you complain long enough and hard enough, good things are bound to happen."
- "People like myself who have always paid more than their share of dues should always get what they justly deserve."
- "The scales of justice must always and ever tip my way. When they don't slant in my direction, I have every right to tick myself off, brood, and obsess about such discrimination."
- "Matters of life and love should always truly and duly be funneled my way - and don't try to tell me any differently!"
- "Because I consider myself to be special, I am therefore to be anointed by having each and every one of my opportunities fall my way."
- "Not only must life grant me opportunities, but it must grant me success in those opportunities, and most assuredly these positive outcomes should come to me rather than I go to them."
- "Noble people like myself should always get their little heart's desire, lest they get themselves upset in a big way."

These assumptions can be keyed in on in a challenging way. By vigorously disputing these original ideas with the following replacement notions, you will begin to unshackle yourself from your self-imposed, self-pitying emotional bondage.

- "Naturally, I would like to get my own way as much as possible. But where is the evidence that I should be the one person in the universe who gets his own way all the time?"
- "Although it would be nice if the universe and people in it would cater to me, I'd best give up such fairy tale expectations in the service of my sanity."
- "If I whine, scream, scowl, moan, and groan enough, that will change things all right - for the worse."
- "Trying to get even with life for not letting me have my milk is like cutting off my nose to spite my face."
- "Certainly I have every right to get myself hung up on my own navel when I don't get my way, but who wants to die with their rights on? Not I!"
- "Better that I make myself open-minded to understand that the world isn't required, nor is it likely going to, bend for me."
- "If I search and research long enough and hard enough, I can probably scare up some opportunities for myself, but opportunity doesn't guarantee success - never has, and likely never will."
- "It would be wise of me to get off my high horse and stop insisting that I'm an elite person and that therefore everything I touch must turn to gold."
- "It's important for my personal happiness to accept the fact that I am not a child anymore and realize that it is high time to put away childish indulgences."

The following are suggestions for thoughts and behaviors that will further assist in relinquishing this woeful state of mind:

1. *View admittance as a sign of strength.* Putting your finger on your self-pity shortcoming and openly labeling it as such is a sign of personality security rather than insecurity.
2. *Come out of the woodwork.* After you get yourself out of the closet by accepting the fact you have this stifling trait, take action by seeking desired advantages in a different context.
3. *Smoke out false pride.* Self-pity can disguise a "keep a stiff upper lip" brand of false pride. It can be one way of hanging on to the notion that you really weren't deficient in not gaining the advantage you sought; rather, it was the universe and others in it who were at fault in not providing (as they must).
4. *Distinguish not liking from not being able to tolerate something.* Because you naturally don't like to go without does not mean you can't tolerate doing so. Lack of tolerance is a contributor to self-pity, and by upping your tolerance level you lessen your pity quotient.
5. *Kick the score keeping habit.* Because the universe runs randomly, it is not wise to itemize how often you gained and how often you lost with the expectation that "now it's my turn to win."
6. *Admit to grandiosity and holier-than-all-ism.* As hard as it might be to acknowledge, admit that by feeling sorry for yourself you are implying anointment: "I, above everybody and anybody else, am the one person in life who should be granted my every wish, for always and ever." The self-pitier really implies that because he or she is better than everyone else, he or she "should" have it better than anyone else. Accepting rather than disclaiming that this faulty notion exists may be a bitter pill to swallow, but will likely strengthen your gut and your resolve to change on the way down.
7. *Tell others.* Openly explaining to others the facts of your self-indulgence and what you are trying to do about it

will likely relieve the stress of having the problem so that you can work more diligently against it.

8. *Avoid double whammy.* Don't go from self-pity to self-blame. Accepting yourself as a person with this common trait will allow you to more freely take a stand against it.

9. *Stop, look, and listen to both the before and after.* Don't whine and scream before the given task that it shouldn't be so hard for you to do, especially because it's so easy for others to accomplish. Likewise, don't crow after your efforts that "it shouldn't have been so hard to complete," especially if it is such a piece of cake for others. Instead, realize that one of the most important assets in life is to understand and accept the reality that you are likely going to be required to work twice as hard as the next person in order to get similar results.

10. *Compliment others.* Try and be happy for those who secured what you weren't able to. Compliment them for their successes even as you feel envy. This direct praise may counter and contain your feeling sorry for yourself.

11. *Compare adversities with others.* Cut out articles from the newspaper that reflect adversities and see if some of them are not larger than yours.

12. *Brainstorm possibilities.* Rather than crying in your beer and pretzels, entertain alternative possibilities to advance your ambitions. Then develop a road map to gain these, as without such a plan, you will likely remain lost in the sea of self-pity.

There's the story of the poker player who, after having been dealt a bad hand, complained strongly to the dealer. The dealer replied, "Shut up and play the game!" Overcoming self-pity will not come from having been dealt a good hand, but rather from trying rather than crying to play a bad hand good. Self-pity takes its emotional toll; it saps your sense of anticipation and participation while holding you back from actively seeking your best interests. Owning up to the facts of what is due you and what is not, concluding that in either case the answer is nothing, leaves you with nothing but opportunity to seek what you would like to own.

Note. From *Feeling Right When Things Go Wrong* by Bill Borcherdt. Copyright © 1998 by Professional Resource Exchange, Inc., P.O. Box 15560, Sarasota, FL 34277-1560.

Threatened Without Feeling Threat: Making Yourself Less Vulnerable to the Fearsome Foursome of the Anxiety Family

Franklin D. Roosevelt said, "The only thing we have to fear is fear itself." Feelings of threat may or may not be related to specific life circumstances. Sometimes the emotional discomfort may take on a life of its own. In order to avoid taking an unwanted event or an undesirable feeling and making it worse, it would be advisable to take on antiexaggerating views. To know what you're up against by finetuning whether your fear is of some specific event or of fear itself would be a good first step toward accomplishing fuller emotional self-control.

Because all humans have emotional cavities, they make themselves remarkably susceptible to the four major members of the anxiety family: conflict anxiety, discomfort anxiety, deprivation anxiety, and disapproval anxiety. Each of these special brands of anxiety is preceded by the presumption "Wouldn't it be awful if I had to contend with conflict, experience discomfort, undergo deprivation, or experience the wrath of others' disapproval." This guide will define and describe each of the anxiety family members, identify irrational beliefs that form their foundation, and offer countering methods of thought that will uproot these faulty notions, while replacing them with more sensible ideas that would better service emotional well-being.

1. *Conflict anxiety.* I believe it was Erma Bombeck who said, "I'd like to be assertive if that's all right with you." Her statement poses a common assertive dilemma. To rock or not to rock the boat: that is the question. Believing that facing the music of differences of opinion with another person will shatter you emotionally prompts avoidance of such discussions. Like all fears, when what one is afraid of is avoided, the fear is strengthened. In that we live in a world of individual differences where it is difficult to get any two people to agree on anything, such avoidances can quickly become a handicapping way of life.

   a. Irrational ideas at the base of conflict anxiety:

   • "I feel terribly uncomfortable when discussing my differences with others so I'll just bury my head in the sand and pretend that they don't exist."
   • "If I face a conflict I might not present my case perfectly well, and that would make me perfectly worthless."
   • "I have to feel comfortable when confronting conflict, so I'll wait until I feel comfortable in doing so or until Hades freezes over before I do so - whichever comes first."
   • "I must say only accommodating, ingratiating things so as to neutralize the power others have over me."
   • "If I approach my differences with another, one or both of our feelings might get out of hand, and all hell might break loose. I'd best avoid the possibility of such a calamity at all costs."
   • "Conflict is such an unpleasant thing that I'm willing to risk everything to avoid it."
   • "If I rock the boat, others might stop thinking that I'm the great person and scholar they presently believe - and that would be unbearable."

b. Countering ideas in the service of emotional well-being:

- "True, conflict is often unpleasant, but conflicts, like other problems, are unlikely to go away just because I look the other way."
- "It's better that I do imperfectly well than not at all when presenting my side of the story."
- "Better that I not feel comfortable in expressing my case, because if I were calm, I wouldn't be as much on my toes mentally."
- "Others have only as much emotional power over me as I give them. Therefore, I can afford to be more direct, informal, and carefree with them rather than thinking I have to find the right ridge on their keister and lick it to cancel out imagined power I wrongly think they have over me."
- "True, if I approach my differences with another, feelings might be made to heat up. False, I would have to let myself get burned by them."
- "Conflict may not be my favorite dance, but it is a reasonably short-run price to pay for long-run self-interest."
- "Patronizing others may win their good graces, but my losses in not affirming my values would likely be much greater than any such fraudulent acceptance."

2. *Discomfort anxiety.* This more general comfort-junkie inclination represents a fear of meddlesome feelings. Feeling out of sorts with one's feeling state and exaggerating the discomfort of such awareness produces an amplifying effect. Viewing with dread actual or anticipated nervous energy will lead to avoidance of the many life circumstances in which such awkwardness might be experienced. This results in a pampering, restricted lifestyle.

a. Irrational ideas that are the building blocks of discomfort anxiety:

- "Wouldn't it be awful if I felt queasy? I couldn't bear the emotional pain and strain of such a happening."
- "Others go along their unruffled way, and I too should be able to control for such constant serenity."
- "What's wrong with me that I can't bring myself to feel tension-free? What a bad person I am for feeling so badly."
- "I must be losing my mind or else I wouldn't be feeling so strange. How horrendous and shameful it would be to end up in a padded cell."
- "I'm in this damned world to feel comfortable, damn it! Any discomfort that creeps in must cease to exist!"
- "Others should recognize my discomfort and find a way to relieve me of it."
- "It's not fair that I experience these emotional complications, and, because I didn't ask for them, some universal force should save me from this awful state."
- "Smile, damn it! Poor me that I don't have emotional self-control at my fingertips. I won't be satisfied until I find that off-and-on emotional light switch."

b. Countering ideas that assist with emotional self-control:

- "I'm not in the world to feel comfortable, but rather to experience it, and that obviously includes a fair amount of discomfort."
- "I don't have to startle myself by my feelings."

- "Causing myself to become a basket case would certainly create mounds of inconvenience. However, catastrophic or belittling it would not be."
- "I, not the rest of the world, am responsible for my feelings generally and my discomforts specifically."
- "Mental health is like dental health: everyone has a few cavities - including me."
- "Better that I not define myself by my feeling states. Though I may consider them good or bad, there is no scientific evidence that my feelings, or any of my other characteristics, constitute me as good or bad. In fact, as far as can be proven, there are no good or bad people, only people with good or bad features, including their current emotions."
- "What is the point of insisting that I be the one person in the universe who leads an ever-present, comforting, womblike existence?"
- "To have emotional containment at my fingertips, though in some ways nice, would not be human."

3. *Deprivation anxiety.* Taking the pout out of going without is the key to combating this discomfort. Rooted in self-pity, this unique brand of self-imposed stress can escape the eye if you let it. Leveling with yourself as to what it honestly would mean to deprive yourself of something tasty allows its detection. Emotional emptiness filled in with pouts and shouts of anguish produces this unpleasant state. Exaggerating the significance of self-sacrifice in the face of indulging in what feels good today - for example, not eating a second helping of food, not purchasing a product that tickles your fancy even though you can't afford it, or not doing something that is fun today because you know you will be disadvantaged tomorrow - brings on this self-affliction.

a. Irrational ideas that force production of deprivation anxiety:

- "Woe is me to be expected to pass on something that feels and tastes so good."
- "In this land of plenty, no one should be expected to turn thumbs down on what they want."
- "I can't bear to entertain the idea of not having something that I want."
- "I just feel too nervous when I ask myself to pass on something I find desirable."
- "I would feel too sick to my stomach to consider not going for it."
- "I've paid my dues and earned the good things in life, so now don't ask me to ask myself to say no to any or all of my wants."
- "Eat, drink, and be merry. That's what life is all about - and don't tell me any different unless you want to get hurt."
- "Lusting after what feels good is so exciting when compared to the monotony of restraining myself."

b. Countering ideas that create self-discipline:

- "I don't have to baby myself when I go without my piece of taffy."
- "Do I want to feel better now by indulging or better over the long haul by not pampering myself?"
- "Little gain without strain."
- "If I eat, drink, and be merry today, I'd better brace myself for having a hangover tomorrow."
- "What could be a better trade-off than the present pain of going without for future gains of happiness and survival?"

- "People who run from the short-run pain of deprivations suffer more discomfort in the long run."
- "The pleasure of the moment often leads to hardship later on."
- "Withdrawal pains suffered from backing away from excesses not good for me are a small price to pay for getting rid of toxic living habits."
- "Better that I call to mind rather than push out of mind long-range negative consequences of my indulgences."

4. *Disapproval anxiety.* The misery equation "others' opinion = me" is what creates this monster of overconcern about what others might be thinking of you. A willingness to sell out one's values in a desperate effort to control for others' favorable review will often end up with you hating yourself for not having enough gumption to be yourself. Foregoing your own expressions with the chance of securing others' liking, and along with it your own immediate comfort, is in contrast to the more mentally healthy axiom of "to thine own self be true."

   a. Irrational ideas that form the foundation of disapproval anxiety:

      - "It is a dire necessity that others always think well of me."
      - "I can't stand the queasiness of being in someone else's doghouse."
      - "Second fiddle by way of someone else's opinion = second class."
      - "Others' thoughts about me are sacred, and therefore I must control favorably for these bigger-than-life items."
      - "What could be more important than another's approval is beyond me."

- "If just one person doesn't like me they will tell others, and before you know it, nobody will like me - obviously a fate that would prove unbearable."
- "Crushed by the weight of others' disapproval is the utter worst way to go."
- "I'm bad whenever others look badly upon me."

b. Countering ideas that lead to acceptance of self in spite of others' disapproval:

- "Better that I examine others' opinions about me without passing judgment of myself by them."
- "Seeking others' approval by abundant patronization of them is a rather hamstrung way to go through life."
- "One sure way to fail is to try to please everyone, and who wants to spin their wheels trying to do that?"
- "True, I have a practical dependence on certain others to the extent that they can inconvenience me if I do not gain their nod. False that I am emotionally beholden to their favorable review before I can accept myself."
- "Although it doesn't feel good to be subjected to significant others' dislike of me, this doesn't mean I have to exaggerate the weight of such discomfort."
- "Gaining others' approval is one of the many important things in life; not gaining any one or even many of them does not have to be considered a disaster."
- "Democracy rules, and when it comes to my own acceptance, I can consider myself to be a majority of one."

Simply knowing that you are the architect of these four anxiety strongholds is a good beginning in becoming the demolisher of them. What goes up can be made to come down. One of the last frontiers of autonomy is to be able to deal with their collective threat by challenging their mistaken ideas about alleged dire needs for harmony, comfort, indulgence, and approval. Vulnerability can be made to turn into victory by expiring your feelings of threat using reason and logic in the service of not letting yourself feel threatened.

Note. From *Feeling Right When Things Go Wrong* by Bill Borcherdt. Copyright © 1998 by Professional Resource Exchange, Inc., P.O. Box 15560, Sarasota, FL 34277-1560.

Doing Someone a Favor By Asking for One: Redefining Assertive Solicitation

Clients often tell me that they have difficulty asking others to do them a favor. I will usually counter their described reluctance by asking, "How do you feel when someone requests a favor from you?" They often report that they feel flattered and appreciative that someone had enough confidence in their ability to fulfill their request and gladness about being able to supply what was asked for. "Why," I then ask, "if this experience is so comforting for you, would you deprive someone else of such satisfaction?" Seeing that just as you feel good when giving to others, they too feel good when they give to you, is a method of understanding that encourages you to actively seek advantages that others can provide - for the benefit of both of you.

Being the Good Samaritan feels good. The helper is helped as much as the helpee. No person can help another without more helping himself or herself. A person is rich in proportion to the riches of kind and deed that he or she gives to others. Given the above paradoxical advantages, making requests of others provides them with an opportunity to enrich themselves. Disinhibiting yourself and asking others what you want from them is an act of kindness toward and benefit to them. To withhold their option to give of themselves is to do them no favor. Doing them the favor of asking for one can be seen as an endorsement of their well-being. It is nice to give and receive; to experience the pleasures of giving, an open request from a receiver is often required.

What's with the timidity? If approaching others for comforts is so comforting for the provider and recipient of service, what is the hesitation about? What are the reasons for throwing cold water on such a mutually beneficial helping connection? The following are blocks that prevent a bolder approach to soliciting others' aid:

1. *Fear of discomfort.* Exaggerating the discomfort of one's own feelings of awkwardness while approaching others creates barriers of contact. Convincing yourself that you would be buried in the avalanche of your own feelings in an asking position will cause you to hightail it from the requester role.

2. *Fear of disapproval.* Insisting upon others' unending approval promotes an unbending, standoffish approach to the idea of striving for others' assistance. Nonnegotiable requirements for the liking of all significant others prompts approval seeking at all costs - including at the expense of pursuing gaining from others what would be in both your best interests.

3. *Fear of rejection.* Thinking that if others reject your request they will reject you encourages a philosophy of avoidance. Viewing others' decisions as an "others' response = me" package deal is a barrier to wheeling and dealing for your advantages.

4. *Presumed payback reluctances.* The score-keeping assumption that asking someone else for a favor will open up the floodgates of their returning your request by making multitudes of their own will cause you to drown in the well of your own inhibitions.

5. *Burdensome ideas.* Believing your requests to be a burden on someone else will result in you taking on the burden of trying to gather all your resources, all by yourself.

6. *Ego pride.* Viewing asking for help as a sign of weakness and a diminishment of self will result in backing away from such a presumed ego-shattering activity.
7. *Double-standard motivations.* Concluding that it is okay for others to ask you for favors, as long as the shoe is on the other foot, brushes on your perfectionistic view of the world.
8. *Dependence on being independent.* Striving to be ultra-self-reliant can take the form of insisting on being an island unto yourself, with no strings or requests made from others attached.
9. *Worry about going to extremes.* Jumping to the conclusion that if you give yourself a dependent inch you will take a dependent mile will cause you to not take any chances. If you think that asking for help from others will eventually lead to turning your life over to them, you will avoid such a possibility at all costs.
10. *Guilt.* Inferring that inconveniencing others by asking for help is bad, and concluding that you would be bad for doing such a negative thing, discourages seeking out others' provisions.
11. *Self-pity.* Demanding that others (a) read your bloody mind and (b) draw you out, pamper you by knowing and granting you what you want from them without you having to ask, and feeling sorry for yourself when they don't, is a 2-year-old's method of proclaiming others' responsibility for you.
12. *Low frustration tolerance.* Vividly describing the alleged agony of getting started in lighting your own assertive fire will leave you far behind in organizing resources of assistance.
13. *Seeking perfect justification.* Trying to establish angelic, noble reasons for making your requests in the first place will result in overexplaining yourself and putting yourself over a barrel in the second place. Not satisfying yourself with a perfect argument for assertively putting forth your

case will block you from making similar requests in the future.

14. *Insistencies on money-back guarantees.* Claiming that if you energize yourself enough to go to bat on behalf of yourself you have to hit a home run each time will prevent you from getting out of the dugout. If you insist on a payoff for each effort of assertion, you will curtail such self-interested activity, knowing that such assurances do not exist.

15. *Faulty self-instructions.* Self-statements that will prohibit doing someone a favor by asking for one include:

- "That's not like me - it's too out of character."
- "I might offend somebody."
- "I couldn't stand appearing so brassy."
- "I'd just melt from my own embarrassment."
- "Others would think I'm weak."
- "I have no right to put someone else on the spot and make a burden of myself."
- "I have no right to make requests and inconvenience others, but they do of me."
- "Others should know what I want without me being required to ask."
- "I have to have a gold-plated guarantee that my request will be honored, or I won't make it."
- "No one likes to be put upon and no one likes people who put upon them, so I'll avoid the disapproval of others by not asking."
- "I feel too out of sorts when I ask of others and I can't stand that brand of discomfort."
- "If my request rubs the other the wrong way, I couldn't bear the conflict that such a scene would create."
- "Oh sure, as soon as I ask him to do me a favor, just watch him bombard me with what he wants from me."

- "I have to remain fiercely independent at all times with all people (because you never know when someone might be watching)."
- "Asking for favors isn't as impressive as providing them (and I have to impress others)."

Heed the following practical suggestions for getting yourself to seek advantages that would be mutually beneficial to you as receiver and to the other as sender:

1. *Appreciate your right to ask.* It's a free country, and you have a right to ask for what you want without prior authorization and without feeling sheepish about it.
2. *Acknowledge others' rights to say no.* Take the burden of proof off yourself by letting others decide whether your requests are unreasonable. They too have freedom of speech and are free to turn thumbs down on your wish as they decide.
3. *Understand solicitation to reflect respect and confidence.* Asking favors from others displays your appreciation of their ability to make the provisions requested from them.
4. *Take on a nonobligatory philosophy.* In addition to others not being obligated to your request, by the same token, if they expect favors from you to piggyback on what they have done for you, it is not necessary that you comply.
5. *Use forced empathy.* Force yourself to lead with their ideas, not yours. Be sensitive to the satisfying feelings that others, as Good Samaritans, have access to by their helping you out.
6. *Minimize self-sacrificial ideas.* Conclude that you are in the world, in large part, to gain advantages for yourself. To sacrifice those advantages that can only be gained from others limits your range of purpose.
7. *Build a case for tolerance.* Use your reluctances to develop emotional stamina. Train yourself to better toler-

ate the discomfort that accompanies asking for what you
want from others without assurance of its delivery.

8. *Put aside friendship and being obligated to not ask as
   being hand in hand.* What are friends for if not to use
   their talents and creativities to mutual advantage? This
   type of positive mutual exploitation is what relationships
   are often made of.

9. *Adopt anticatastrophizing, antiexaggerating views.* See
   that all hell will not break loose under the discomfort and
   possible backfiring of your outreach efforts on behalf of
   yourself.

10. *Utilize massed practice.* Don't pussyfoot around; consis-
    tently use your persuasive powers to get others to comply
    with what you want from them. Repeated action on
    behalf of yourself will help develop an immunity to your
    concerns about such activity.

11. *Replace faulty self-instructions.* Mistaken ideas that
    prompt a breakdown in bridging your own best interests
    can be disputed with the following self-explanatory ideas:

    • "The fact that it has not been a consistent part of my
      character to actively seek from others what I wish
      from them does not mean that I can't often do so
      now."

    • "What's more important: what others think of me
      and my request or what I think? Methinks, what I
      think is."

    • "Some people will likely admire me for the same
      things others will dislike me for, including my for-
      wardness."

    • "True, I may make myself feel awkward about asking
      for what I want. False, that such discomfort would be
      beyond the realm of tolerance."

    • "I, as do others, have a right to make and refuse
      requests. Asking or giving is each in its own way an
      inconvenience. Due to free will, anyone can refuse

my request that might prove to be an inconvenience to them."

- "I'd best not expect others to pamper me and cater to me by knowing what my little heart desires without me assertively asking."
- "I don't have to know tomorrow's answers about my requests of today - and I don't necessitate favorable assurance of my requests before I make them."
- "No one can be put upon by me unless they agree to honor my asking."
- "I can use my discomforts about conflicts specifically to work toward developing more of an immunity toward discomfort generally."
- "The likelihood that others who abide by my requests would expect me to go along with theirs doesn't mean that I would be mandated to do so."
- "I don't have to impress others about anything, in cluding how independent of their favors that I may or may not be."

Help a person out by actively seeking provisions from them. You and they stand to benefit. Identifying and promoting the mutual advantages of assertive solicitation are kind, not unkind, and convenient, not inconvenient methods of servicing relationships. He who hesitates denies and loses joint satisfactions that come from forthrightly joining with another in practicing the belief that it is nice to give *and* receive.

Note. From *Feeling Right When Things Go Wrong* by Bill Borcherdt. Copyright © 1998 by Professional Resource Exchange, Inc., P.O. Box 15560, Sarasota, FL 34277-1560.

Double Whammy: Arrogance and Reverse Arrogance - Two Sides of the Same Perfectionistic Coin

Many people are like my client Mary (a pseudonym), who, when questioned what advice she would give to a friend with a similar problem as hers, quickly replied that she would first suggest self-forgiveness. Yet Mary was far from giving herself the benefit of the not-being-perfect doubt. Rather than follow her own suggestion of compassion, she was putting herself down for having the problems that she did. She was practicing what she later called "double whammy" and "reverse arrogance." I will define what these terms mean, the background ideas from which they are created, and countering ideas to work against these problem-about-the-problem tendencies.

Double whammy means giving yourself a problem for having a problem. A multiplying effect is produced when you hassle yourself for having a problem or exaggerate the significance of your concerns. Putting pressure on yourself via self-put-downs or catastrophic emphasis on your discomfort will mass-produce the original concern. Until you take pressure off yourself for having problems in the present it will be unlikely that you will make fewer errors in the future. This self-inflicted aggravation is often seen in the following self-statements:

- "It's awful that I overreact so."
- "I *have to* stop making myself so upset."

- "What an idiot I am for acting so idiotically."
- "I know better, so therefore I should act better."
- "Damn me for acting so foolishly."
- "I have no right to act so badly."
- "I can't stand feeling so upset."
- "There's no reason for me to be this way, and therefore I must not ever act so badly."
- "I can't tolerate it when I cope with my problems so poorly."
- "This is too much - I can't bear all of my problems."
- "I couldn't possibly coexist with my problems and discomforts - I must get over them."

These perfectionistic types of notions will make you a prime candidate for double emotional trouble. They can be substituted with the following coping ideas that build a case for emotional containment:

- "I find my problems to be objectionable and hopefully correctable, but in the mean time I'd best find them disappointing rather than disastrous."
- "It would be far better to cease making myself so upset. However, although I will shoot for the bull's-eye of doing what is far better, I'd best see that I, like other humans, am not always going to hit dead center."
- "I sometimes act idiotically, but that does not qualify me for being a village idiot."
- "I do know better and I will try *my* best to put my knowledge into action; however, I doubt whether I'll ever do *the* best in my efforts."
- "Due to free will and human limitations, I have a right to be wrong. I am wrong in being wrong - don't get me wrong - but to state that I don't have this right is to say I don't have a right to be human."
- "I can hold myself accountable for my errors without blaming myself for making them."

- "I'd best build a case for action rather than overreaction; for deliberation rather than desperation; for acceptance instead of anguish about my concerns and discomforts."
- "If I settle my carcass down in the first place, I will be better able to combat and contain my problems in the second place."
- "I'm an imperfect person in an imperfect world, flanked if not surrounded by imperfect people. I'd best view this as a sometimes grim, but not too grim, reality."
- "I can take my problems and discomforts with me. I don't have to make it a sacred mission to get rid of them before I put one foot in front of the other."

Arrogant-acting people feel fear and anger. They believe themselves to be inferior to begin with and are afraid that others will find this out. They use anger in an attempt to intimidate others into thinking they are strong when they really feel weak. They lack compassion for others. They take on a "holier-than-thou" manner. They invent ego heavens. They engage in psychological one-up-personship. Feelings of superiority are worn on the lapel of the arrogant-behaving person, betraying their inner anxieties about themselves.

Reverse arrogant-acting people experience guilt or depression and lack compassion for themselves. They put themselves down in a futile attempt to drive themselves toward perfectionistic ambitions. They present an "unworthier-than-all" appearance. They invent ego hells. They express psychological one-down-personship. They seem to be specialists in berating themselves for their flaws. What they fail to see is that their own ongoing stance of apologizing for themselves really masks a lack of self-humility. Their reverse arrogance is seen in their overdone response to their own imperfections. Others they are quick to forgive, but themselves, seldom. Permissiveness with others is their trademark; giving themselves some emotional slack is beyond their comprehension. They do not exaggerate others' mistakes, yet cream themselves about their own.

Arrogant-acting people are easy to spot. They strut like peacocks about their presumed superiority. They keep their nose in the air in an effort to put themselves above others. People who have reverse arrogance are not very visible. They outwardly come on like humble pie. Inwardly they expect more of themselves than of others because they believe themselves to be above the ranks of human imperfection. The masses they can forgive; it is for themselves that they lack tolerance. They express themselves in quiet, other-forgiving but self-damning ways, reflective of their pious manner. They are quick to lighten up on others, but because of all their perfectionistic splendor, are unwilling to loosen up on themselves. They carry with them ideas that reflect this reverse-arrogant position statement: "It's okay for others to err; they can be forgiven. After all, they are just mere mortals anyway. However, because I am such a noble soul, I am not allowed luxuries of grace and acceptance." Unlike displays of arrogance, which are obvious, what you see in the ultra-tolerant, reverse-arrogance antics is not what you get. What comes across as seeming never-ending tolerance of others is really an intolerance for one's own fallible nature.

Arrogant-acting people make no bones about it. In word, manner, and deed, they dramatically express what they view to be their exceeding stature. Their "I'm better than you" philosophies are seen in the following expressions and mannerisms:

- "You're beneath me."
- "I'm better than that."
- "There's more dignity to my lifestyle than to yours."
- "I'm better because I have more education (money, special skills, etc.) than you do."
- "I'm a winner, you're a loser."

- "I'm a success as a person - you're a failure as a person."
- "You're dumb compared to me."
- "I've had better experiences than you and I'm a better person because of it."
- Purposeful inattentiveness while listening to someone.
- Raising of one's eyebrows in a condescending manner as a way of expressing disapproval of another.
- Sighing or snickering about someone else's views in a manner that implies you're better than they are.
- Intentionally cutting someone else off in the middle of a sentence.
- Slyly teasing someone about something you know he or she is self-conscious about.
- Consistently acting in unreliable and undependable ways that express your taking the other for granted.
- Gossiping about another's faults in an effort to exalt yourself.
- Expecting others to do the "dirty work" because you think it's beneath you.
- Excessively talking about the successes of your children when you know the other hasn't experienced near as fortunate parent outcomes.

A reverse-arrogant stance reflects the following ideas and mannerisms:

- "Other people can make mistakes, but I can't."
- "I'm too good to do the stupid things others do."
- "I was born on the right side of the tracks. You can't expect much from those born on the wrong side."
- "I'm too smart to make common errors."
- "I have a reputation to live up to."
- "I must never tarnish my sacred image."
- "Others are to be pitied for their shortcomings; I am to be blamed for mine."

- "When others make mistakes, it's a disappointment. When I make mistakes, it's a disaster."
- Sheepishly looking at the ground in the aftermath of a mistake.
- Overapologizing for your errors, for example, "I'm REALLY sorry."
- Using dramatic facial expressions to express displeasure with self.
- Avoiding others who have knowledge of your blunder.
- Displaying a hunched-up, tightened body posture that reflects your self-blaming beliefs about your error.

Carly Simon sang, "You're so vain, I'll bet you think this song is about you." If you are so imperfectly vain that you think this essay is about you, pack up the extra emotional baggage you have been carrying around with you, deposit it elsewhere, and see if this doesn't supply a breath of the fresh air of self-acceptance. Lessen your tendencies to hound and bound yourself by your self-blame for and your overreaction to your original problems. Curtailing double whammy and both vintages of arrogance tendencies can be done by taking on the following ideas that indicate more tolerance of self and others:

- "We're all in this together, and nobody is better than anyone else."
- "Mistakes don't make the person."
- "Compassion begins at home, and the best way to draw closer to my social group is to lighten up on myself for my mistakes. This will make it more convenient for me to do the same with others."
- "Pulling a blunder is not bigger than life and the worst of all possible crimes."
- "Perfectionism is like trying to find a needle in a haystack that doesn't exist."

- "Even though I wasn't born equal, I was born free, including the freedom to not rake myself over the coals for my shortcomings."
- "Trying to put on the psychological cosmetics to impress others is more trouble than it's worth."
- "There are no winners or losers, successes or failures - only people who sometimes win and succeed or lose and fail."
- "My behavior doesn't demean, discredit, or stigmatize me any more than others' behavior does them."
- "True, some people have more advantages than others and are therefore in these ways better off. False that these assets make any of these people a better person."
- "There are no subhumans or superhumans, only humans."
- "To error is human, to blame often appears to be even more human, but is really (in)humane because you end up putting undue pressure on self and others."

These statements suggest the value of avoiding all appearances of the evils of passing judgment on humans. These very strong natural self- and other-rating game tendencies naturally lead to problems. The double-whammy, dual-arrogant mentality is the same hearse with a different license plate. Both represent desperate attempts to prove oneself rather than be oneself. In the end they poison efforts to live happier and kill a more clearheaded approach to your vital interests. Like life in general, if you don't rebuke these two timing inflections, you will be unlikely to get through your upsets emotionally alive.

Note. From *Feeling Right When Things Go Wrong* by Bill Borcherdt. Copyright © 1998 by Professional Resource Exchange, Inc., P.O. Box 15560, Sarasota, FL 34277-1560.

Defeatism and
Its Conveniences

"I can't do it." "I can never make it wash." "Every time I try I fail." "I never get chosen." "I always come away the loser." These are all "I'm beat before I start so I may as well not try anyway" slogans of people who view themselves as automatic losers. Parents, teachers, supervisors, and motivators of all sorts harp against a defeatist attitude and its disadvantages. Yet, prematurely giving up seeking goals and ambitions is often allowed to be a dominant force.

A defeatist attitude is looking at one's relationship with self, others, and life and concluding, "This is the way I, others, and life have always been; this is the way I, others, and life are; and this is the way we are always going to be." Defeatism doesn't consider the possibility of change. It is as if defeatist-acting people find victory in defeat, would have a problem about not having a problem, and therefore justify their inaction.

This guide will take a further look at the irrational beliefs that lie behind such a predetermined, negative approach to projects and goals. More importantly, it will identify countering thoughts that will allow you to get yourself beyond throwing in the towel before the game even gets started. Motivation by temporary convenience excuses present action and has some short-term advantages. Yet, with all the preachings against taking on defeatist values and their long-range negative consequences, one might easily assume that negative thinking would not be practiced as often as it is. Why this is not the case can be found in the following reasons why defeatism is expressed as an avoidance mechanism.

1. *Comfort of the moment.* Immediate comfort can be gained by rationalizing that there is no use in even trying. That way, the stress and fatigue that go along with stalking personal goals can be avoided. An instant rush of relief is made to override the strenuous effort required to get started.

2. *Perfumes the failure experience.* At least in admitting defeat early, it is experienced on the terms of the loser. Some consolation is gained from knowing that you failed because you decided not to try rather than from your active deficiencies.

3. *Escapes others' disapproval.* Staying on the sidelines rather than putting yourself into the game is less likely to bring any flaws in your performances to the attention of the disapproving crowd.

4. *Hole-in-the-doughnut thinking.* Pessimistic attitudes that highlight the hole in the doughnut, rather than the doughnut itself, naturally give vent to defeatist tendencies. Overlooking the possibility of success is convenienced by such negative-slanted thinking.

5. *Indecision is supported.* Fence riding or consideration of alternatives without commitment is regained from halting at the brink of goal-directed movement. Temporary satisfaction is gained knowing that at least you didn't make a wrong decision to plunge into something that may have been over your head.

6. *Pacifies deprivation anxiety.* Pouting that is often made to accompany going without can be stalled by not requiring yourself to be deprived of the tasteful activity that your goal-seeking activity would have replaced. Depriving yourself of such an immediate pleasure is viewed as just too much to ask of yourself.

7. *Escape from inconvenience anxiety.* Demands for a hassle-free life, free of frustrations and annoyances, can motivate you to call on beat-before-you-start notions in the service of honoring this childish insistence for a continuation of a womblike existence.

8. *Avoids the shame-of-it-all fallacy.* Not recognizing that in the event of a public blunder one would not be required to induce shame promotes rationalizing inaction in the service of avoidance of this unpleasant emotion.

9. *Flight from feelings.* When meeting a challenge, especially for the first time, one often feels like a fish out of water. Rather than confront such feelings of insecurity by making contact with the proposition, defeatist notions can be given to justify not putting yourself through such awkward feeling experiences.

10. *Keeps the dream of certainty alive.* Emotional dependency on knowing that tomorrow's outcomes will be successful, merry, and bright will forestall forging ahead with constructive goals - backed by destructive, defeatist excuses, of course.

11. *Irrational thinking.* Defeatism is supported by ideas that make it seem easier to beg off trying to put your best foot forward. These include:

   - "Things never go right for me, so why even bother to try?"
   - "It's too much of a hassle to try to get started, and it's not worth it anyway - let me rest me some more."
   - "If I'm going to fail, it's going to be on my terms - by not even trying to get out of the dugout."
   - "Just as sure as I'm a foot high, I know I am going to fail and that others will disapprove and smirk if not laugh at me for failing. I couldn't stand it and therefore must avoid these calamities."
   - "Getting in there and pitching makes me feel too nervous, especially because I know I'm going to lose anyway."
   - "Until I can predict victory over defeat, I'll keep myself in the neutral zone. I can tolerate being in the middle of the road but not on the side of it."

- "I couldn't stand making the personal sacrifices called on to succeed, especially because I know my efforts, as usual, can only turn out for naught."
- "Because I'm only capable of making wrong decisions, I won't make any at all - dumb me!"
- "To be inconvenienced is bad enough, but to know that it can only lead to falling on my face again is even worse."
- "It's just so much easier to sit here and do nothing, especially knowing that the best I could ever do would be to come away the loser again."

Defeatism and its motivations by short-range conveniences can be countered by the following suggestions:

1. *Confess to comfort-junkie outlooks.* Admit that you cop out because it feels good at the moment you do so. By admitting defeat before you try, you justify not trying. As a result, you feel better but get worse by encouraging the habit of avoidance.
2. *Lead with self-compassion.* Just as important as owning up to your defeatist ideas is accepting yourself in spite of them. By not putting yourself down for your fatalism you clear the runway for taking off on the next step.
3. *Practice countering self-sentences that dispute irrational ideas.* Correct original irrational thoughts by fresh ideas such as:

   - "The fact that something once happened, like failure, doesn't mean that it has to continue to happen."
   - "The fact that something hasn't happened, like success, doesn't mean that it never will happen."
   - "The past does not have to continue to have an indefinite influence on my present efforts."
   - "Keep an open mind - and keep in mind that it's not easy to take the easy way out."

- "Present pain is a small price to pay for future success."
- "Having not succeeded up until now doesn't include future possibilities for success."
- "When I base future outcomes on past experiences of failure, I promise myself to fail again. I'd best avoid this self-fulfilling promise."
- "The line of least resistance, in terms of any present comforts gained by giving up before I start, is really the line of most resistance, because I will miss out on greater long-range comforts."
- "Trying again and failing again is better than not trying again."
- "It's better to be 0-100 than 0-0, because then I can learn things from my failures that can be applied toward possible future successes."
- "It would be better to rid my vocabulary of everlasting words such as "always," "never," and "every time." I can replace them with "so far," "to this point," and "up until now." This will permit me to make more flexible and well-though-out decisions about whether to forge ahead with my goals."
- "Life is tentative and ever-changing and is best approached with sustained passion. Better that I approach it with similar permissiveness and persistence."
- "You win some, you lose some. Better that I increase my chances of winning some by trying than to guarantee that I lose all by not trying."
- "Even if I failed 100% of the time, I still would be 0% beholden to others' disapproval for doing so."
- "Taking my anxieties with me defeats the conveniences of avoidance."
- "Better that I stay away from the impossible dream of knowing tomorrow's answers today, because that makes it all too convenient to defeat myself before I start."

- "Inconvenience is not the end of the world, even if it turns out to be a more permanent disadvantage."
- "It's often not convenient in the long run to take the convenient way out."
- "If I want to succeed more often, I'm probably going to be required to fail more often."
- "The entry fee for success is failure."
- "The promised land may have a few mountains in front of it, but I don't have to mountain climb over mole hills about them nor assume that I can't climb such obstacles."

4. *Begin to reverse your immediate pleasure patterns.* Start to appreciate that it's not easy to take the easy way out, and plan your future accordingly. Press into action behaviors that show a concern not so much about how they result in you feeling now, but about their impact on your feelings for the rest of your life.

5. *Give yourself heavy doses of consequential thinking.* Directly ask yourself: "Where does this type of thinking get me?" "How does it help/hinder?" "What would be a better way to think and act?" Confronting yourself about the advisability of current thoughts and actions can set in motion rational alternative, optional methods of thought and deed.

6. *Avoid the self-fulfilling promise.* Defining failure before it happens guarantees it. Avoid being true to your prediction by more open-mindedly letting actual experience fill in the blanks of outcome.

7. *Purposefully encounter failure, discomfort, and disapproval.* Deliberately test out your hypothesis that you can't stand failure, couldn't live with discomfort, or would be unable to survive others' disapproval. Do this by purposefully putting yourself in social circumstances that may result in these disadvantages occurring. Meet these fears on your terms and see if you don't start to develop an immunity to them.

8. *Distinguish "can't" from "won't."* List all the things you tell yourself that you can't do because of lack of resources. Honestly see if there are not many on that list that you *won't* do because of lack of gumption.
9. *Escalate unaccustomed feelings until you become accustomed to them.* Bring on queasy feelings associated with strenuous effort and the possibility of repeated failings and see if you can bear with and learn to not startle yourself by such out-of-sorts experiences.
10. *Explain to others.* Inform others about your lacklusterness and the flimsy, convenient excuses behind it. Do so as a means of better targeting your self-defeating thoughts and behaviors for destruction.

Rationally admit defeat if you have actually lost, but don't permanently irrationally admit defeat into your philosophy of living. By not allowing doomsday, fatalistic, and finalistic thinking to enter your approach to life, you defeat defeatism and its disguised conveniences - much to the convenience of your long-range happiness and survival.

Note. From *Feeling Right When Things Go Wrong* by Bill Borcherdt. Copyright © 1998, Professional Resource Exchange, Inc., P.O. Box 15560, Sarasota, FL 34277-1560.

White Lies Versus Black Truths: Twelve Reasons It Is Not Always Practical or Advisable to Be Honest

A man forgets his wife's birthday. He explains, "How do you expect me to remember your birthday when you never look any older?" His response illustrates the intention of this guide, to raise some doubts regarding the question "Is honesty always the best policy?" Not having a love affair with total honesty can be a loving act, can save your love life, and can bring you many other advantages. George Washington's biographer tells us that as a child, Washington said, "I can't tell a lie. I did cut it [the cherry tree] with my hatchet." Such a dramatic display of honesty appears to have been a noble act for the man later to become President, but is such openness best for all people, in all situations? I doubt it.

George Bernard Shaw stated, "All great truths begin as blasphemies." In light of our culture's alleged sacred priority on being truthful in relationships, to suggest to the contrary fits Mr. Shaw's prerequisite for truth. When does a white lie become a black truth? When being honest does not contribute to your long-range happiness and survival, that's when. The following list of 12 disadvantages that can result from being truthful illustrates when a white lie might do better in promoting your long-range happiness and survival than a black truth. Each had best be considered when weighing the pluses and minuses of expressing your position. Lying is often considered to be an immoral act. In its broader sense, immoral means to hurt a human being. Exposing yourself to the following disadvantages that can stem from being truthful, you may be acting immoral in the sense of hurting the human being that is yourself. Perhaps George Washington's principle declaration doesn't often fit; perhaps George Bernard Shaw was right.

Potential hazardous fallout from embracing unquestioned honesty:

1. *Backfires into practical disadvantages.* Saying the wrong thing at the wrong time can result in you being on the outside looking in to your (former) job or marriage. If you have a sneaking suspicion that your work supervisor or your marital partner doesn't like it when you voice certain opinions, you'd best use self-interested discretion in doing so.

2. *Others take it personally.* If you have a hunch that the recipient of your statement is going to interpret it as being against him or her and an attempt to do him or her in, it might be better to reserve comment for the good of the order. This is especially so when the other has the leverage to withhold advantages from or to make life annoying for you.

3. *Others' potential emotional overreaction.* When dealing with those who have been known to make themselves into drama majors when you don't tickle their ear, it might be more trouble than it's worth to put all your cards face up on the table. The black truth emotional fallout cure might be worse than the white lie disease.

4. *Discourages compromise.* Strongly stating that you think your way is better may encourage a counter unbending response from others. Mutual dialogue can often be better encouraged by a less black-and-white, more shade of gray, flavor to your presentation.

5. *Retards relationship development.* Patronization in the service of confronting to the detriment of the relationship had best be the order of the day. Many relationships will not stand the test of provocation. Extending associations are often better accomplished by agreement and accommodation. Whether you do so with a straight face or not is beside the point.

6. *Disadvantages the development of high frustration tolerance (HFT).* Self-restraint is a difficult thing. Telling yourself that you have to be (brutally and totally) honest because you can't stand the discomfort of not letting all your bright ideas hang out all at once strengthens existing difficulties in tolerance. Putting your foot on the brakes rather than the gas pedal about the points you want to drive home will likely aid you in becoming a more tolerant-acting person.

7. *Discourages behavioral trade-offs.* "I'll scratch your back if you scratch mine," the bread and butter of many successful relationships, will more likely be frowned upon if you come to your declarations knowing they are likely to rub the other person the wrong way.

8. *Conveniences further digging in of heels.* The more you openly counter others' views with your honest appraisal, the more likely they are to even more strongly oppose you. This is especially so with those who, by the strength of their convictions, give off the impression that they have a monopoly on truth. The more you forthrightly contest their stronghold of ideas, the more strongly they are likely to resist considering what you have to say.

9. *Increases potential for conflict, stress, and strain.* Direct statements, although reflecting reality, can make a rocky road rockier. Most people tend to make themselves defensive and combatant when their views are questioned by contrary appraisal. Not rocking the boat in the service of treading smoother relationship waters fits with William

James's statement: "The art of being wise is the art of knowing what to overlook."

10. *Misses the pleasures of agreement.* Many things that people take issue with one another about aren't worth arguing over. Losing the joys of accommodation can be a large price to pay for sticking to your opinionated guns.

11. *Discourages others' openness.* You are likely to learn less about others if you make it a point to often challenge their values. Honest, contradictory observations can throw cold water on desired communication.

12. *Loses beneficial relationships.* If taken too seriously, your comments will result in others taking their ball and bat and going home. Losing a relationship means losing the advantages that accompany it. Don't cut off your nose to spite your face when you think you will have more to lose than gain in standing up and being counted.

When deciding whether to let all the truth hang out or smudge it a little bit, consider the following thoughts that precede white lies as opposed to those that come before black truths. Note that those ideas associated with white lies are more rational (evidence for and better contributing to one's long-range happiness) than those irrationally (cannot be proven and block personal happiness) connected with black truths.

Thoughts that lead to white lies:

- "I don't have to prove my point."
- "The possibility that I will feel better if I express my opinion doesn't mean I have to - especially if doing so will get me worse results in the long run."
- "It's a rare bird who takes the truth in stride. Let me see if I'm dealing with such an animal before I decide to open up."
- "Life is too short to create conflicts that I can just as well - in fact better - do without."

- "I'd best be totally honest about what I consider to be my vital interests, but only if I'm reasonably certain that I won't do myself in by my directiveness."
- "If I know that my associates are allergic to certain foods, I won't feed them those. Likewise, if I know that they will make themselves have an allergic emotional reaction to what I consider to be the gospel, I'd best not entice them with those views."
- "Live a little, give a little - agreement in the face of disagreement."
- "Finding shades of gray is often the right thing to do."
- "White lies can be kind and loving; black truths can be cruel and unloving."
- "Do I want to feel better now by shooting my opinionated wad or do I want to feel better for the rest of this relationship's life by seeking out the good in what I believe to be bad?"
- "Present pain of restraint for long-range gain of relationship extension."
- "The short-run sacrifice of choosing my words carefully is worth the long-run gain of keeping relationships on track and running smoothly."
- "Do I want to be a live dishonest coward or a dead honest hero? (I only regret that I have but one life to give for myself, so I'd best choose the first option!)."

Thoughts that lead to black truths:

- "I have to say exactly what is on my mind, and I can't stand it when I don't."
- "I owe it to him to level with him 100% regardless of the cost."
- "She deserves to know exactly what I think of her. She's got it coming."
- "If I muffle my tone and blunt my message, others might think I'm weak, and that would be terrible."

- "No guts, no glory - and I need glory, regardless of how gory it gets."
- "I have a right to my totally honest opinion, and I'm going to exercise this right, even if it kills me."
- "Come hell or high water, I cannot bring myself to back down from expressing what I think is right."
- "I'll ram my ideas down his throat and teach him a lesson he will not soon forget."
- "If I go along with everything she says, she will think I'm a stupid puppet, and that would be too much to bear."
- "I've got too much pride to agree when I disagree - only wimps do that."
- "Restraining yourself is dangerous and hazardous to your health, so I'd better fully express my views in an unrestrained way."
- "How upset they get themselves about me telling them the whole black truth, and nothing but the truth, so help me (as) God, is their problem."

Nathan Hale said, "I only regret that I have but one life to lose for my country." The human dilemma in the crossroads of many circumstances of disagreement is whether to be a live coward or a dead hero. Giving your one life to your country is a noble thing to do. Sacrificing your long-range best interests for the gratification of the moment is quite another thing. Perhaps it is those who refuse to come down from their truthful perch who are more psychologically wimpy. This would especially be the case with those who resist backing off because they would see themselves as weak or would be fearful others would view them disapprovingly if they went out of their way to accommodate the situation rather than conflict with it. Black truths are often opted for over white lies due to personal insecurity. It takes a secure person, well grounded in self-acceptance, to relinquish false pride and use the tolerance required to be more interested in extending and benefiting from a relationship by being wrong than in disrupting and disadvantaging it by being right.

These ideas are not an attempt to build a case for passiveness and nonassertion, but for using discretion about what is likely to be the right choice with this person, in this situation, at this time. Hold your ground on vital matters, but give strong consideration to long-range practical realities. Choose a white lie or a black truth with your eyes wide open so you don't get the black eyes that often follow black truths that could have been prevented by white lies.

Note. From *Feeling Right When Things Go Wrong* by Bill Borcherdt. Copyright © 1998, Professional Resource Exchange, Inc., P.O. Box 15560, Sarasota, FL 34277-1560.

Pain in the Neck,
Burr in the Saddle,
Thorn in the Side:
Containing Annoyances

Keeping an upper hand on your emotions does not mean eliminating them, nor the life circumstances that contribute to them. Feelings of frustration following disappointments related to shortcomings in yourself, others, and life's conditions had best be expected and accepted. This guide is about acknowledging molehills but not making mountains out of them; how to recognize disappointments but not amplify them by throwing gasoline on them. Just as steamed is not the same as cooked, displeasure does not have to be increased to emotional disturbance. Feelings can be better regulated, toned up or down, depending upon the mindset that you bring to your inconvenience. The human tendency to exaggerate the significance of events, though powerful, is not binding. With the right methods and practice you can learn to leave bad enough alone and not unduly increase your emotional temperature.

The feeling states on the next page are not only healthy but helpful in that they make you aware that something is amiss in your life and serve as a motivator to regroup your resources. These yellow caution flags of dissatisfaction do not need to be amplified into dangerous red flags of disturbance.

Displeasure	Concern
Sadness	Wonder
Irritation	Frustration
Sorrow	Inconvenience
Regret	Deprivation
Annoyance	Disappointment
Discontent	Disenchantment
Apprehension	

Examples of pains, burrs, and thorns to be contained:

- Being informed by school or other community authorities that your child has committed a misdeed.
- A friend who doesn't show up at an agreed-upon time and place.
- The book or money you lent out doesn't get returned when expected.
- Your picnic gets canceled due to bad weather.
- You get passed over for promotion.
- Your child talks back to you.
- Your mate abruptly changes his or her mind about an agreed date.
- Relatives drop by unannounced at an inconvenient time.
- A check you wrote is returned, marked "insufficient funds."
- You find yourself being unjustly criticized.
- You pull a public blunder.
- You voice an opinion and the other person snickers.
- You are told "no" to a reasonable request.
- You hear of gossip that has been told about you.
- You kindly ask for someone else's opinion and he or she refuses to give it.
- The person from whom you are expecting a decision seems afraid to make it.

- You offer a workable compromise and the other person takes a hard-line, refusing stance.
- Someone makes unrealistic expectations of you.
- You give a compliment and the other person doesn't accept it.
- You want to discuss something and the other person wants to argue about it.
- Your sincere apology isn't accepted.

You get the picture. You get what you don't want or don't get what you do want. You put your best foot forward and end up standing there flatfooted while getting them stepped on. To deny being influenced or affected by such annoyances is to deny being human. When out on a limb with seemingly no place to go, the temptation is to press the panic button. Instead, see that being influenced or affected by negative happenings is different from disturbing yourself about them. Acknowledge distaste for something but don't escalate disappointment into disaster. Use the following methods for not upping your emotional ante:

1. *Use emotional regulation coping ideas.* Strongly and persuasively tell yourself rational ideas such as:

   - "Disappointments are not disasters!"
   - "It's not bigger than life!"
   - "Don't get yourself bent out of shape!"
   - "Don't flip your wig about it!"
   - "Don't climb the walls over it!"
   - "Molehills are not mountains!"
   - "Lighten up - it's not the end of the world!"
   - "Cool your jets!"
   - "Part of life, yes! Bigger than life, no!"
   - "This matter is important, not all important!"
   - "I find this to be surprising, not shocking!"
   - "This is bad, not catastrophic!"

- "Tough beans this time around!"
- "If first I fail, I can try again!"
- "Expect the unexpected!"
- "Something to be concerned about, not consumed by!"
- "This is difficult to accept, not devastating!"
- "This is unfortunate and unpleasant but not terrible, awful, or horrible."
- "This is very much a hassle, but not a horror!"
- "This is a handicap, not a disability!"
- "This is painful but not a killer!"

2. *Dispute irrational ideas.* Add to using the brief coping ideas earlier by more completely challenging and changing faulty philosophies that prompt exaggerations and overreactions.

- "Where is the evidence that, when faced with a difficult life circumstance, I must become highly and visibly disturbed about such a reality?"
- "Where is the proof that if my ambitions don't turn out the way I strongly want them to I must overwhelm myself with upset?"
- "Why must I not be frustrated, deprived, and inconvenienced, and why must I hoot and howl when I am?"
- "Why can't I bear utter frustration, hassle, and annoyance, live to tell about it, and possibly learn something from it?"
- "Where is it written that life is not for lessons, and why must I not learn a few - the hard way?"
- "How is it revealed that the too-numerous-to-mention, unfair-and-unjust pains, burrs, and thorns in the universe should not exist, and why ought not I be required to pay the dues of experiencing the handicaps of those burdens? In my nutty head, that's how it is revealed - better that I take a second look at my off-base conclusions!"

- • "When something seems threatening and fearful, why do I have to overfocus on it as if it were a foregone conclusion that the worst will occur?"

3. *Find humor, even in the most unlikely places.* Something doesn't have to be funny for you to find humor in it. Because a sense of humor is a sense of proportion, it can help make sense out of the most annoying of circumstances. In doing so, it serves as a safety valve for not blowing things out of proportion.

4. *Reduce expectations.* Expect yourself to be frustrated by your own, others', and life's limitations. That way you will make yourself less inclined to fan the flames of emotional upset when they inevitably appear. As Albert Ellis, founder of rational emotive behavior therapy, has often said: "It doesn't say hassle-free on your birth certificate."

5. *Seek repeated pleasures.* Itemize the hundreds of potential pleasures that you could experience, and actively and daily program some of them into your life. That way you will likely be too busy pursuing your enjoying interests to be concerned about more petty things.

6. *Respect the law of averages.* See that many of the things that you worry might happen or might continue happening are actually unlikely to do so. Expected burdens oftentimes never come, and when they do, they usually eventually go. Playing these odds over in your mind and giving yourself the benefit of the doubt can be comforting.

7. *Project yourself ahead of time.* Visualizing the long-term significance of present frustrations will likely lead you to understand that they aren't going to last forever. Picturing how you will feel about present irritations a week, month, or year(s) from now will encourage a more hopeful view of coming out of, though not snapping out of, your problem.

8. *Especially challenge your "I-can't-stand-it-itises."* At the core of escalating annoyance into emotional disturbance is low frustration tolerance (LFT). Making yourself feel undisciplined about the amount of tolerance required to bear with rather than blow up discomfort is a significant force in setting boundaries on unwanted emotions. Convincing yourself "I *can* stand what I don't like" will produce the high frustration tolerance (HFT) required to better manage your emotions.

9. *Curtail absolutistic thinking.* Human disturbance is the result of demandingness, protesting against the negative realities of life. Insisting in an all-or-nothing, black-or-white way that disenchantment not exist - for example, "This *should* not be," "Others *must* change," "I *have to* do better," "This is not the way it is *supposed* to go," "Life *ought to* be different" - pumps up emotional disturbance. More permissive views that stay with acknowledging disappointment in the face of lost goals and preferences - for example, "I wish things were different, but it's not the end of, nor the worst thing in, the world that they are not" - will deflate upset.

10. *Find the good in something bad.* At a minimum, you can use your present annoying state of affairs to work on your mental health by better accepting and tolerating it. Not that there is a silver lining behind every storm cloud, but adversity, just like success, has its advantages; that is, what you learn from pushing yourself past current difficulties can be put to use in similar circumstances in the future.

11. *Give yourself exposure therapy.* Paradoxically expose yourself to annoying situations until you develop more of an immunity to them. Force yourself to talk to people you don't enjoy associating with, face rather than tiptoe around conflicts, state opinions that are likely to be frowned upon, and do other things that will result in discomfort. Meet these displeasing matters on your terms and see if you can't in the end beat them.

12. *Tackle one annoyance at a time.* Don't get ahead of yourself. Cope with immediate concerns as they rear their ugly heads; you can't deal with trouble until it gets here. Jumping ahead to what "could," "might," or "may" happen, turning possibilities into inevitabilities, will likely end up with you being afraid of your own shadow. The net result of such future overconcern is likely to be you doing a little bit of a lot of things but not too much of one thing while watering down your problem-solving efforts in the process.

Come to expect and come to terms with negative realities that aren't going to go away. Pains, burrs, and thorns will affect and influence you, but that doesn't mean that you have to disturb yourself about them. Tighten up your view of what hassle means for you so as to tone down your response to such aggravations. Dispute their impact, don't despise their existence. Cultivate a tolerant view of annoyances by planting rational views about them so as to better contain and lessen their absorption in your life.

Note. From *Feeling Right When Things Go Wrong* by Bill Borcherdt. Copyright © 1998, Professional Resource Exchange, Inc., P.O. Box 15560, Sarasota, FL 34277-1560.

When One Size Doesn't Fit All: Golden Rules and Their Contradictions and Contraindications

George Bernard Shaw said, "The golden rule is that there are no golden rules." Golden rules are those ideas believed to be ordained, carved in granite, that their holder absolutely insists apply to all people, all the time, in all situations. Such compelling, rigid, nonnegotiable ways of thinking hold that yesterday, today, and forever human response is to be the same; that this is the way life has been, is, and will forever be. The problem with such everlasting thinking is that it doesn't allow for one of the most obvious things about humans: their individual differences. Such sacred notions come in the form of "shoulds," "musts," "have to"s, "got to"s, or "ought to"s. Attempts to establish such ruling universal laws result in the ruler placing unrealistic demands on self, others, and/or life. The three basic all-purpose irrationalities that rational emotive behavior therapy tries to abolish are: "I must be perfect," "You must treat me perfectly," and "Life must be perfectly easy." Relinquishing this tripod of insistencies will likely promote more personal well-being and interpersonal accommodations. What Shaw was implying was that if we look at our lives, including our relationships with others, in more flexible, open-minded ways, we will better contribute to our long-range happiness and survival.

"Thou shalt have no other values before mine" is the message of golden rules and of those who cling to such seeming almighty, answer-to-everything declarations. This guide will seek to go about amending such dyed-in-the-wool, black-or-white, all-or-nothing ideas as a means of mending your emotions. Disadvantages of thinking that "my way" is "the way" include the following:

1. *Makes the solution into the problem.* Each this-way-or-that insistence brings on increased stress and tension between sender and receiver. High and mighty demands on others will likely increase friction between associates.
2. *Promotes "holier-than-thou-ism."* Commanding that others see and do things your way signifies a top-dog mentality that leaves you believing that you really do rule the roost and that such a perch makes you better than others.
3. *Discourages creativity.* Expanded ideas are unlikely to flourish in the midst of single-mindedness.
4. *Encourages bigotry.* Intolerance and outright fanatic attachment to a cause or creed often is the end result of stubborn opinion.
5. *Often results in anger, rage, or fury.* Frenzied, self-centered beliefs often lead to aggressively retaliating on those who dare to think differently. At its extreme, such malicious conduct has led to the attempted annihilation of individuals, groups, and nations.
6. *Creates the illusion of universal standards.* Unreasonable proclamations are rooted in the false idea that there are universal laws and that the holder of such notions is the universal enforcer of them.
7. *Abolishes free will.* Others are told to restrict their free will and become instilled with "my will" in the application of extravagant commands.
8. *Implies anointment.* Holders of inflexible values are really saying that an almighty force has taken over their lives and is giving them permission to take over yours.

9. *Doesn't allow for human imperfection.* Humans have pushed themselves off the beaten path and probably will continue to do so, whether it be their own idea or someone else's, even when it would be in their best interest not to do so.

10. *Has undemocratic overtones.* It is unbalanced and undemocratic to demand that others abide by your values.

11. *Promotes loss of practical advantages.* Restricting your thought options will likely lessen the advantages that could be gained from more general brainstorming in search of keys to success.

12. *Leads to poor sportsmanship.* Fair play, workable compromises, and mutual problem solving are lost when rigid thinking rears its ugly head.

13. *Piles on layers of false pride.* Ego boosters that provide a false sense of confidence are created while trying to inflict one's noble, angelic ideas on others.

14. *Encourages a personalized worldview.* Holding fast to the idea that you know all the answers to all the world's problems and then discovering that others choose not to comply with them sometimes results in a "woe is me," me-against-the-world conclusion. "What's wrong with me that I cannot get others to jump upon my sacred bandwagon?" is a self-statement that often follows reality killing the dream of worldly compliance to your value system.

15. *Sparks condemnation and punitiveness.* Demanding that others not stand in the way of your saintly ideals can easily slip into damning and condemning those that do have the gall to oppose your views.

16. *Brings on social group standoffishness.* Know-it-alls are in a class by themselves and will remain there due to their obnoxious arrogance.

17. *Plants the seeds of magical thinking.* Fanatical jubilance manufactures a sense of power that is rooted in the childish equation that if I just jump up and down long

and loud enough, my words will magically, but surely, be heeded.

18. *Triggers defensiveness in others and dependency in self.* A guarded stance is often prompted in others when it is demanded that they toe the mark of your dictates. Dependency on their doing so comes from believing you will lose your lofty perch if, heaven forbid, they don't come along for the ride.

19. *Frequently ignites the reverse golden rule.* Frenzied efforts to get others to abide by your golden rules can easily lead to a way of thinking typified by the statement "Others should do unto themselves as I do unto them." In other words, because you have busted a gut to demonstrate your point of view, others must return equal effort in understanding and accepting your views: "If I try hard to administer my way of thinking, others have to try hard to adopt it - and damn them if they don't."

20. *Doesn't acknowledge and respect individual differences.* Perhaps the major contraindication of golden rules is that they assume everyone is the same, with like tastes, preferences, goals, values, and inclinations. Even in the most basic golden rule - "Do unto others as you would have them do unto you" - human variance gets lost in the shuffle. At the risk of committing blasphemy, this most hallowed golden rule of them all assumes everyone is the same. As such, it borders on self-centeredness in that it implies that others are merely an extension of your values. A view that would be more considerate of others' preferences would be "Do unto others as they would have you do unto them." This wider range perspective provides the advantage of walking at least a mile in others' moccasins while more fully appreciating that one size doesn't fit all.

Following is a list of rules of demands, dictates, and "golden rules" that put unnecessary strain on individuals and their relationships, followed by countering rules of preference that prompt emotional relief.

DEMANDING "GOLDEN RULES" THAT PUT PRESSURE ON SELF, OTHERS, AND LIFE GENERALLY. All imply a desperate necessity, life-depends-upon-it outlook - the "have to"s, "musts", shoulds", "got to"s, and "ought to"s.	COUNTERING RULES OF PREFERENCE THAT REDUCE STRESS AND STRAIN. Wishes, wants, preferences, or likes that signify a nondesperate, nondependent, nondictatorial approach.
"I *have to* find a way to communicate more with my children."	"At times I *would like* to communicate more with my children, and, although it is disappointing when I can't, it certainly is not the end of the world."
"I *must* actualize myself and realize all or at least most of my potential."	"I *would like* to and I *hope* to do well with the personal resources I have, but I can accept that the sky is not the limit in terms of human potential and therefore I may often come up short."
"I have always been kind and friendly to my family and therefore they *ought to* always treat me with no lapses in similar kindness and consideration."	"Perhaps my fondest *wish* is that my family treat me acceptingly and exceptionally kind - but that is their decision, one I can both live with and not hold against them."
"I *should* go to church and *should* visit grandmother after church, every Sunday."	"Some Sundays I will likely *want* to go to church and visit grandmother, and some Sundays I likely won't. Let me distinguish between the two and meet my preference on each occasion."
"I've *got to* find an easier way to do this difficult task."	"It sure *would be better* to find an easier way, but in the meantime, a little elbow grease never hurt anyone."

DEMANDING "GOLDEN RULES" THAT PUT PRESSURE ON SELF, OTHERS, AND LIFE GENERALLY. All imply a desperate necessity, life-depends-upon-it outlook - the "have to"s, "musts", shoulds", "got to"s, and "ought to"s. *(Cont'd)*	COUNTERING RULES OF PREFERENCE THAT REDUCE STRESS AND STRAIN. Wishes, wants, preferences, or likes that signify a nondesperate, nondependent, nondictatorial approach. *(Cont'd)*
"Others on my team have *got to* cooperate with and understand me."	"It sure is *preferable* when others play ball with me and are sensitive to my wants, but the show can be made to go on even when they don't."
"I *should* always turn the other cheek."	"Sometimes it is in my best interests to roll over and play dead, and other times I would *do better* to openly protect myself."
"I *should* feel guilty for making a mistake, especially repeated ones."	"*Better* that I feel sorrow and regret for my errors so as to motivate myself to correct them, but I certainly don't have to condemn myself for making them."
"I *must* never change my mind."	"Sometimes it is *desirable* that I change my mind and sometimes it is *desirable* that I not do so."
"The world *should* always be fair and I *ought to* always get what I deserve."	"It *would be better* if the world were fair and full of deservingness - sometimes. In truth, I would not wish to get what I deserve all the time!"
"I *should never* accept compliments too openly."	"Where is the evidence that I must not enthusiastically accept compliments, if I *wish* to?"
"I *must never* question authority."	"When it's in my best interests to question authority, I *may wish* to do so."

DEMANDING "GOLDEN RULES" THAT PUT PRESSURE ON SELF, OTHERS, AND LIFE GENERALLY. All imply a desperate necessity, life-depends-upon-it outlook - the "have to"s, "musts", shoulds", "got to"s, and "ought to"s. *(Cont'd)*	COUNTERING RULES OF PREFERENCE THAT REDUCE STRESS AND STRAIN. Wishes, wants, preferences, or likes that signify a nondesperate, nondependent, nondictatorial approach. *(Cont'd)*
"I've *got to* always fight fire with fire, deal with others' anger angrily, and fight back at any costs."	" 'Monkey see, monkey do'; trying to make two wrongs into a right is often *not the preferable* approach."
"I *ought to* only say nice things, *always* responding the way others want me to."	"*Sometimes* it is preferable to patronize others, and *sometimes* it is not."
"I *have to have* certain advantages."	"I will not hesitate to seek my *wants,* but such niceties are merely nice, not necessary."
"Bad things *ought not* to exist in life."	"Good is better than bad and therefore *more desirable*, but that does not prove that a mixture of the two ought not to exist."
"I *have to* be comfortable and feel like doing something before I do it."	"I would *prefer* to be in the comfort zone before I put my best foot forward - but I can also take my discomfort with me."
"Others *should* do unto me as I do unto them."	"Others can treat me the way they damn well please; after all, I don't run the universe yet!"
"Do unto others as you would have them do unto you."	"Do unto others as they would have you do unto them."

The more forcefully you attempt to apply golden rules, the more tarnished they become. Trying to shove inflexible commandments down your own or another's throat doesn't consider free will, human limitations, and individual differences and is therefore a contradiction to the realities of the human condition. Humans are not clones of one another. Amending seemingly superior regulations rather than forcing those issues holds better promise that a more permissive means of creating emotional slack within yourself and in your relationships with others will be gained. Rather than try to fit a round peg into a square hole, see that there is a direct, hand-in-glove relationship between your willingness to amend frozen, golden judgments and better mending your personal and interpersonal well-being.

Blind Alleys, and Why You Would Be Lost Without Them

William Faulkner once said that if he had a choice between feeling pain and feeling nothing, he would choose to feel pain. Faulkner poses a common human concern: to avoid living in an emotional vacuum at all costs. Almost anything is better than life becoming like watching the paint dry - or being at an undertakers' convention following the announcement that the longevity rate has just gone up 10 years! While I was watching television at my mother-in-law's home, she inquired as to whether an open door was an obstacle for my viewing. In jest I responded, "Yes, it is another obstacle - and I don't know what I would do without them."

This guide contends that there are many valuable by-products to failure, frustration, and disappointment. Seeking and losing can provide meaning and opportunity. Not only does vital absorption counter do-nothingism, but it supplies other advantages as well. Success can be found in the most unusual places, including when you come up short in your goals. Finding your way home often requires navigating a few blind alleys. Good benefits that would be lost by not going down bad dead ends include the following:

1. *Builds commitment confidence.* Faith in your ability to forge ahead is a lasting advantage in the service of increasing the likelihood of getting more of the advantages and fewer of the disadvantages in life.

2. *Develops scavenger and survival skills.* Learning to make the most out of immediate frustration allows you to squeeze more juice out of a problem-solving turnip in the long run.

3. *Fosters emotional self-reliance.* Even when you come up short in efforts to succeed you will likely lengthen and strengthen your independent abilities. Learning that you can always count on yourself is a reassuring discovery.

4. *Provides a basis for comparison.* It is easier to appreciate where you are now when it can be contrasted to where you have been. As one client put it: "Thoughts of where I have been push me forward."

5. *Signals accessibility to others.* Getting into life's flow and continuing to pitch regardless of outcome lets people know that you prefer involvement over avoidance.

6. *Strengthens feelings of accomplishment.* Many desire a feeling of accomplishment without (a) accomplishing anything or (b) ever failing. Because anything worth doing is worth doing poorly, accomplishment has its investment of perspiration and frequent failings as entry fees.

7. *Constructively structures time until you can convince your ship to come in.* Seizing the opportunities that are to your liking often are required to wait, and so what better thing to do in the meantime than act as a participant observer in your life circumstance?

8. *Disputes irrational beliefs.* The best way to change a faulty notion is to act against it. Happiness-blocking ideas such as "Failure is shattering," "I must succeed," and "I can't bear losing out" are actively disproven when it is seen that you are living proof that you can survive your failings.

9. *Builds high frustration tolerance (HFT).* Going to the well and consistently coming back empty can increase the emotional stamina out of which eventual success is built. Neither Rome nor achievements are built in a day.

Rather, patience as virtue can be produced from immediate setbacks and then put to use in future strivings.

10. *Tilts the chance factor more in your favor.* Pasteur said, "Chance favors only the prepared mind." What better way to learn how to increase the chances of finding your way home than to rule out a lot of blind alleys first. The persistence factor, even when stacked up against odds, can often be made to rule the roost in the end.

11. *Salvages dreams that inspire hope.* Perseverance is a mechanism for keeping dreams alive. This is followed by hope increasing life's meaning.

12. *Distinguishes between losing the battle and winning the war.* Even a series of defeats does not constitute a loss. Recognizing that there is always a tomorrow following loss is an elegant form of self-encouragement.

13. *Builds and builds upon a philosophy of challenge.* Going to bat for yourself, even when there are two strikes against you, cultivates a nonavoidant manner of approaching life.

14. *Separates being down from being out.* Getting yourself up for the next task after being down from the last one has major advantages. Keeping your fight rather than turning to flight will keep you moving onward and perhaps upward toward your projects.

15. *Introduces actions as speaking louder than words.* If a picture is worth a thousand words, then actions are invaluable. Making decisions that hit home drives home important messages that prompt believing in yourself as an action-oriented person who gets things done.

16. *Fights against pampering, whining, and pouting.* Babying yourself before testing out the waters, or pouting about going without in the aftermath of failure, enlarges emotional anguish. Better that doing rather than stewing become the byword in warding off these infantile tendencies.

17. *Practices a good habit.* Trying can be made to have a life of its own. Effort fed upon itself builds emotional momentum that when harnessed often gets good results.

18. *Makes you more likely to discover the truth.* Plato said that the truth will win out in the end. However, it is unlikely that you will hit the nail on the head until you become more practiced at swinging the hammer. The more you search, the more clusters of factors you will be able to piece together to form your finished product.

19. *Invites compassion.* Putting one foot in front of the other in spite of multiple falterings conveniences a more permissive, accepting view of self.

20. *Defeats procrastination.* When slacking off is replaced with massed practice, the philosophy of "putting off until tomorrow what has already been put off until today" is replaced with "Nothing works but working" and "Doing gets it done."

21. *Heightens alertness.* A keener sense of anticipation of and participation in life's activities is accomplished by repeatedly putting some teeth in your ambitions.

22. *Can lead to the cutting edge of new ideas.* Peeling away layers of failure today will often bring you to the brink of creative methods that could be tomorrow's breakthrough.

23. *Highlights adventuresome living.* Willingness to travel uncharted territory promotes a life of vim, vigor, and vitality associated with taking the high road.

24. *Encourages a scientific outlook.* Emotional health can be defined as taking on a scientific attitude. Testing out your hypothesis with no assurances for success will reveal a no-lose database. Whether you discover information that is helpful or not, the experience will be significant because learning what doesn't fit for you is just as important as what does hold true.

What would life be like without obstacles and blind alleys? Probably predictable, with less meaning and narrowed self- and other-understanding; boring at best. Mark Twain attributed much of his creativity to his painful case of gout. Nagging frustrations help us to appreciate more fully happier times and in this brings joy as a possibility. Such discomforts can sensitize one to the perspiration out of which many vital absorptions are formed. Where does it say one has to succeed to create a highly meaningful existence? Home is where the head and heart are. Diligently trying to find your way there affirms a no-lose existence that you would likely be lost without.

Note. From *Feeling Right When Things Go Wrong* by Bill Borcherdt. Copyright © 1998, Professional Resource Exchange, Inc., P.O. Box 15560, Sarasota, FL 34277-1560.

Trial and Error
Without Putting Yourself
On Trial

There is a difference between risky and at risk. There are times when risk isn't risky. In fact, what is often viewed as risky really isn't. This guide will review what is and what isn't at stake when trying to gain more of life's advantages. This is an important distinction to make in that until you understand that you are not at risk you are likely not to try. This is not to imply that you don't stand to lose practical advantages if you try and fail, but it is to say you won't lose your value to yourself. Most people beg off the attempted effort required to chance achieving a given result because they fear losing face and therefore conclude that possible failure is shattering. Not venturing to seek a job promotion, make a new social contact, or take assertive action with a critical associate are examples of silent attempts to spare the personal discredit that is presumed to automatically accompany failure.

Mental health is related to having a scientific attitude. That includes gathering evidence about your experiences to see if your data collection supports or contradicts your original hunch. Such hands-on information gathering includes a lot of trial and error but will be unlikely to take place if you believe yourself to be on trial. As long as you believe that your failures are answerable to your ego, you will trap yourself by thinking that success or failure defines you as an individual.

The most successful people fail the most, because they appreciate that anything worth doing is worth doing poorly. They know that many things learned in failure may become able to be put to good use later on. If you try, you are likely to succeed sometimes. If you don't try, you will always fail. Like casting for fish, the more you cast, the more likely you are to eventually get a strike.

If you believe something to be risky, you will correctly see that if you fail, you will be forced to go without something. Such a possibility will create a healthy concern that will likely motivate you to ward off such deprivation. If you incorrectly believe that you are at risk, you are likely to consume yourself with panic about the possibility of losing everything - including yourself. Putting yourself on trial in judging yourself by the outcome of your project efforts will likely result in the following possibilities:

1. *Absolute avoidance of the possibility of failing by not trying.* Those who make failure sacred have this as their motto: "If I try I might fail; if I fail I'll be a no-good failure; so I'll sidestep being no good and a failure to boot by not trying." The result of this avoidant philosophy is that little will be ventured, gained, or discovered in such a tiptoeing-around lifestyle.

2. *Results in disorganized attempts to problem solve.* Bind yourself up emotionally via self-proving desperation and you will likely approach your projects in a highly stressed, clumsy way. Self-evaluation, where you put yourself on the line along with your outcome, makes for inefficient, bleary-eyed efforts. Startling yourself about the possibility of failure will increase the chances of bringing on what you startle yourself about.

3. *Encourages guilt or despression.* Self-judgments in accord with good successes ("Therefore I'm good") and bad failures ("Therefore I'm bad") will prompt you to feel guilty or depressed when you either fail to get started

on your goals to begin with or try to achieve your ambitions but fail.

If trial and error lead to self-improvement, while putting yourself on trial results in self-downing, what state of mind and mood would do better in terms of deliberate rather than desperate goal seeking? Surrendering the following five key irrational ideas by disputing their content will likely prove helpful:

1. *Irrational belief that bears surrendering:*

   "If I do something, I have to do it (perfectly) well or I may as well not do it at all."

   Dispute/challenge: "Can it be proven that I have to be skilled at something before I do it?"

   Answer· "No, such a notion cannot be proven."

   Countering rational beliefs:

   • "Anything worth doing is worth doing poorly."
   • "If it were accurate that people had to do something well before they did it, little would get done, because skill ordinarily follows, not precedes, practice."
   • "It's better to do than to do well. In fact, I may learn more from failing to do well than from doing well."
   • "Life is for lessons; let's see how many I can learn - including, perhaps especially, from trying and failing."
   • "Although failure is a hard knock, many longstanding lessons can be learned in the school of hard knocks."
   • "If I fail, I can be glad I'm failing, because that means I'm learning something that I may be able to put to good use later on."

- "Trying and failing means I'm sending myself a message that I believe in the value of my own existence enough to go to bat for myself."
- "Trying has a life of its own; succeeding or failing is often secondary."
- "Trying can be habit forming, and what better habit is there to form?"

2. *Irrational belief that bears surrendering:*

"Failure is shattering and demeaning and therefore is to be avoided at all costs."

Dispute/challenge:　"Is it really accurate that failing is catastrophic or disgraceful?"

Answer: "There is no validity to this idea."

Countering rational beliefs:

- "If failure were shattering and demeaning, then everyone would be shattered and demeaned, because everyone fails."
- "On the contrary, failure can be enlightening and add to personality well-roundedness."
- "Success or failure does not define me as a person."
- "If I avoid failure, I avoid life and miss the meaning my efforts can contribute to it."
- "Granted, in some ways I may be worse off if I fail, but I won't be a worse person."
- "I do my failures, but I am not my failures."
- "Acknowledge and hold myself accountable for my failures, yes; condemn myself for making them, no."
- "Better that I give my efforts a trial run. Better yet that I not put myself on trial relative to them."

3. *Irrational belief that bears surrendering:*

"I have to have a guarantee that my efforts will at least partially pay off. Without such assurance I couldn't stand to proceed knowing that I might falter and my pride and image along with me."

Dispute/challenge: "Is there really a universal standard that says I have to know tomorrow's success answers today, could not tolerate the uncertainty of not knowing, or that how I view myself is dependent on whether I succeed or fail?"

Answer: "There is no universal standard to support any of these premises."

Countering rational beliefs:

- "If it's guarantees I seek, I'd best look in a different world."
- "Come to think of it, life would be boring if it possessed the surety, certainty, and orderliness that I foolishly and childishly demand."
- "Even though I may have more time than money, I can well afford to wait on tomorrow's answers."
- "Concern about self-image is directly tied in with my insisting that I impress others. I'd best give up such foolishness or I will end up trying to prove myself to all people, all of the time."
- "I can leave my ego pride on the doorstep rather than take it along with me to tomorrow's outcome."

4. *Irrational belief that bears surrendering:*

"I have to know that others will cooperate with and support my efforts, as any such public opposition to the contrary would be shameful."

> *Dispute/challenge:* "Where is it written that it is necessary that others lend me a helping hand with my vital interests and that any or all outpourings of disapproval would be shameful?"

> *Answer:* "There is no evidence that would favorably reflect on this absolute assumption."

Countering rational beliefs:

- "Others' affirmation of my efforts is highly desirable but not a necessity."
- "Others' disapproval will likely bend my mood to the point of disappointment, but I would not have to let it break to the point of disaster."
- "Trying and erring cannot cause shame, only self-belittling conclusions could do that, and I have the free will to not make that happen."
- "I do not have to explain my shortcomings to anyone, and to make myself insistent on doing so will breed utter frustration."

5. *Irrational belief that bears surrendering:*

"I have to feel comfortable before attempting a project, and any stress or tension along with it must be avoided at all costs, especially since others might notice my discomfort and judge me as a bad weakling because of it."

Dispute/challenge: "Can it be proven that discomforts and others' judgments of me for them must be avoided at all costs?"

Answer: "There is no proof that such a comfort zone requirement exists."

Countering rational beliefs:

- "I can unshackle myself from my fears of discomfort by taking them with me."
- "Some discomfort is an advantage because it helps keep me on my toes."
- "I don't have to intimidate myself by my own nervousness or about the possibility of others negatively judging me by it."
- "Lusting after comfort will only encourage me to avoid new opportunities, in that when I do anything for the first time, I will likely feel awkward."
- "Discomfort along with others' disfavor is often the entry fee for expanding my experiences. I can pay now by staying with the discomfort, or I can pay later by missing out on what I might learn."

Trying to avoid failure by not trying - now that's risky! You risk losing all that could have been gained and learned from trying. There is always a chance factor when trying to succeed. There is no chance factor when you halt yourself at the brink of your efforts. Inaction brings a foregone conclusion of business as usual. To head off such a stalemate, don't put yourself in a courtroom where you and/or others are the judge and jury of your emotional destiny. Leave your ego on the doorstep rather than allow such judgments to override your best emotional interests. Plead yourself not guilty by reason of sanity.

Note. From *Feeling Right When Things Go Wrong* by Bill Borcherdt. Copyright © 1998, Professional Resource Exchange, Inc., P.O. Box 15560, Sarasota, FL 34277-1560.

And Justice for All:
Doing Justice to Yourself
By Not Overreacting
To Injustice

"What's fair is fair" is a slogan that cannot be universally applied. What might be an advantage to and fair for someone else may result in unfair disadvantage for you. You may have worked harder than the competition and still not gain the promotion; you may have written a manuscript with a higher potential to contribute to social significance and never get it published; you may have prepared yourself exceptionally well in your parenting role only to discover that your child has a mind of his or her own that leads him or her down the garden path of social conflict. Justice? What's just? For whom? Is there really such an animal?

This guide will discuss rational ways to manage injustice. Turning on the evening news or glancing at the front page of a newspaper easily documents some of the realities of a world filled with injustice. Because of the abundance of injustice, the value of developing a philosophy of emotional containment in the face of getting the short end of the stick is an important field of study. To give an uncaring, lackadaisical, limp-hand emotional response to unfairness would not, at one extreme, be in your best interest. Neither would, at the other end of the emotional spectrum, a hurtful, angry, aggressive response bring service to your objectives for rational living and long-range happiness and survival.

Unfairness often exists for unspecified reasons. There is only so much room for so many people to be at the right place at the right time. Due to our competitive nature, there is just so much room at the top. The universe runs in a random, impartial fashion. The laws of average and nature assure that people will not be born equal; some will have more advantages than others. For these reasons, in looking for justice one is likely to go down a lot of blind alleys. To say the least, injustice is a given part of the human condition. To not accept its existence in your own backyard, instead insisting that mercy and justice must always triumph so as to shelter you from discomfort, is to (a) invite self-pity, hurt, anger, and depression, and (b) result in you taking a bad situation and making it worse in the midst of your upset.

With unfairness as par for the course in human existence, what can be done to prevent yourself from giving yourself an emotional disturbance problem about the problem of injustice? The following suggestions will assist you to roll with the punches of inequity that hit below the belt. Although we are not born equal, we are born free, including a free will to think what we want to think, regardless of circumstances. By willfully adopting the following perspectives, you will not shield yourself from injustice, but you will likely better assure lessening its impact on your life.

1. *Be fair to yourself.* When circumstances and others in it are not being fair to you, it is all the more reason to be fair to yourself. What better way to be fair to yourself than to make a determined effort to not disturb yourself about someone or something you have no control over?
2. *Avoid self-evaluation.* Resist the temptation to judge yourself by your difficult situation. See that no one can demean you but you, and that the fact that disfavor in your life is bad does not mean that you are bad. Your bad exposure to injustice does not equal you, it is an experience you have.

3. *Research the advantages.* Honestly do some homework by seeking out possible long-range benefits from short-run deficits. The worst experiences can result in the best learnings. What is gained later on can be more appreciated when compared to what was earlier lost.

4. *Don't presume anointment.* Appreciate your uniqueness but don't define yourself as special. Such a declaration makes it convenient to jump to the conclusion that because you are so special, some universal force is to provide you with special favors of fairness and deservingness. Special implies anointment, and by disbelieving these twin towers of alleged mercy, you take the wind out of your insistence sails before they begin to operate.

5. *Identify and dispute irrational ideas.* Track down faulty notions related to your childish demands that justice must prevail. See if they don't reflect incorrect notions such as, "The world has to be fair to me and justice and mercy must always triumph in my life"; "I should be the one person in the universe who is at least consistently treated justly by others in and by the conditions of life"; "Everything in life that I want, I should be able to have (especially if I've worked hard for it), and everything that I don't want ought not exist (and I can't stand it when it does)." Then, question these pearls of self-invented wisdom - in other words, uninvent them by substituting, "Where is it written, and where did I ever get the dumb and bum idea, that the world was made for me and has to be fair to me?" "Why must I only experience comfort and fairness in life? Am I not here to experience life, including a fair amount of discomfort and unfairness?" "Where does it say that I have to get a return on my best-effort investments, and why do I have to moan and groan, wimp and whine when I don't?"

6. *Rejoice about the unjust component of life.* Be glad you get what you get and not what you deserve! Chances are you wouldn't always appreciate getting what you deserve.

Also, be glad that the world doesn't run in orderly cycles, making it impossible to predict outcome by effort. Not knowing whether justice or injustice will dominate is part of what makes life interesting. It also can spell relief when you discover that you didn't get what you believed your efforts or lack of efforts deserved.

7. *Especially zero in on self-pity.* A woe-is-me attitude is difficult for most people to own up to. Yet, until it is admitted to, you will continue to cry over milk spilled, possibly through no fault of your own. In your own no-nonsense way, strongly explain to yourself, "I don't have to cry in my beer when justice does not rule the roost (and I'll be fair to myself by not doing so)."

8. *Contribute to making others' unfair world fairer.* Donating your time, energy, and money to those less fortunate than you are can rekindle your appreciation for the ways that life's ball has bounced in your favor.

9. *Apply the brakes sooner, rather than later.* Don't let your demands that justice conquer all your potential hardships get out of hand. The quicker you own up to the facts of your overreaction to injustices, the sooner you will be able to act rather than react against them. Promptly putting your foot on the brakes of your low tolerance for discomfort allows you to prevent the effect of pyramiding emotional upset.

10. *Give up magical, impossible dreams.* The fact that you get presents at Christmas doesn't mean that there is a Santa Claus. Things may break to your advantage, but that doesn't mean that there is a fairy godmother, leprechaun, or rabbit to be pulled out of the hat that will always tip the scales of justice in your favor.

The purpose of acclimating yourself to inevitable injustices is not to whitewash or wonderfulize about its effects. Neither is it to overkill or awfulize the results of its presence. Rather, it is to go into the teeth of its realities, however sharp, and not allow yourself to be emotionally eaten alive by them. This healthy perspective can curtail the effects of injustice on you presently, so that you can better enable yourself to do justice to yourself by being happier in the future.

Playing Possum:
Understanding and Overcoming
Disguised Ignorance

Getting past acting like you don't know what you do know can be a valuable expedition. Many a bright idea has been lost by putting on the mask of ignorance rather than putting the best foot and idea forward. Disadvantages to self and social group can be avoided by being willing to go out on a limb about what you believe to be right. Those who hesitate to assert their position are lost - as are ideas that could make a difference for the better. Why do people purposefully wear the mask of ignorance when better results might be gained? What can be done to overcome tendencies to lie back in the weeds and blend in with the woodwork when you have something to say? This guide will examine this laid-back problem by identifying its causes and cures.

Whether it be a student who knows the right answer but doesn't raise his or her hand when the teacher is looking for a volunteer to pipe up; an employee who plays dumb when his or her supervisor is seeking answers to questions he or she is familiar with; a committee member who doesn't offer his or her knowledge in the midst of the group's brainstorming; or someone in social conversation who pulls away from rendering an opinion that from his experience he has found to be true, shying away from disclosing knowledge as a quiet way of pleading ignorance is a frequent error of omission. Such purposeful hesitancy and avoidance can be explained in the following ways:

1. *Exaggerated view of consequences.* When the possibility of putting your foot in your mouth is viewed as devastating, standing up and having your opinions accounted for will be made to be too risky.
2. *Exaggerated view of discomfort.* When thinking about the possibility of saying the wrong thing is associated with exceptional feelings of queasiness and awkwardness, withdrawal from any circumstances where this could happen is likely.
3. *Fear of conflict.* Thinking that what you have to say might conflict with others' noble ideas, and believing what an absolute horror that would be, will sandbag verbal assertiveness.
4. *Fear of success.* Fear that if your ideas are viewed as valuable others will therefore expect you to come up with good ideas in the future will prompt you to back away from any statements to begin with.
5. *Fear of disapproval.* Claiming a dire dependence on others' liking will prompt you to avoid the possibility of what you have to say rocking the boat of others' acceptance.
6. *Minimizing your contributions.* Pleading humble pie by throwing cold water on the possibility that you might have ideas of merit is a way of rationalizing inaction in a manner that reflects personal insecurity.
7. *Avoidance of shame.* When the risk of public disclosure of an idea that could misfire is seen as bigger than life, buttoning your lips overrides personal expression.
8. *Guilt.* Believing that putting yourself down would follow uttering a misguided opinion will lead to sweeping your thoughts under the rug rather than risk voicing them.
9. *Fear of appearing superior.* Dreading that others might think you a braggart if you openly identify your fund of knowledge will prompt you to put to waste rather than use your ideas.

10. *Perfectionism.* Waiting for the perfect time, place, and delivery before you spill the beans of your views will indefinitely stall putting your ideas out on the table.

It only takes one to play the game of possum, and it only takes one to stop. Overcoming this special form of social avoidance can be accomplished in the following ways:

1. *Make the invisible visible.* Admit to, rather than fool yourself about, the existence of the problem. Until you make clear to yourself that you have the problem of disguised ignorance, you won't get your foot in the door to solve it.
2. *Get started immediately.* There is no time like the present. Hesitation will strengthen your fears; action will weaken them.
3. *Become a two-fold scientist:*

   • Dispute your irrational beliefs about what expressing yourself means for you. Search for new ways of looking at this old problem until you find them. Ask yourself, "Where is the evidence that if what I have to offer on the topic doesn't come out right or is frowned upon by others the world would come to an end?" "Can it be proven that I could not bear any emotional discomfort I would bring on while exercising my freedom of speech?" "Where is it written that I would be proven to be a schmuck if I came across schmuckily?" See that it would indeed be unlikely that the cosmos would be significantly affected if you did falter; that in all probability you would not die from the discomfort that might accompany your assertions; and that if you did a second-class job of expressing yourself, you wouldn't be demoted to second-class citizenship.

- *Get a database.* Give yourself homework assignments that would behaviorally test out your hunches
regarding your abilities at and possible consequences
of self-expression. That way you base your decisions
to go or to not go forth with your statements on fact
rather than fiction. The best way to examine whether
a belief stands the scrutiny of scientific inquiry is to
act upon it. Experience is the best teacher. Learn
rather than guess for yourself your potential to present
yourself, to cope with a less-than-perfect presentation,
and to accept yourself regardless of outcome.

4. *Don't short-change your ideas.* Don't throw cold water
on your life experiences as they reflect your views.
Downgrading your ideas leads to assuming that others'
opinions are better than yours. Understand your perspective to be unique, and appreciate and express it as such.
5. *Heavy doses of "I" statements and "you" questions.*
Practice daily, "I think _____, what do you think?"
Such sending of and soliciting for opinions allows you to
rehearse your expressional skills while developing an
immunity to discomfort.
6. *Develop philosophies of adventurousness and challenge.*
Boldness can be exciting and challenging. Persistently
viewing your efforts at letting your opinionated cat out of
the bag as such can serve as motivation.
7. *Counter movements.* Make it a point not simply to practice going public with your opinions but also to give
them the hard sell. Use persuasive methods in attempting
to influence others as to the merits of your views. Such
added practice and intensity may help you to more quickly appreciate the value of what you have to say and your
ability to say it.
8. *Look for free opportunities.* Don't backpeddle by looking
a gift horse in the mouth. When you overhear others
giving their views on a given topic, identify those parts

you agree and disagree with. Zero in on each as a means of acting against your bad habit of keeping your ideas to yourself.

9. *Appreciate the warmth of the light at the end of the tunnel.* Envision how good it will feel as you train yourself to be less hesitant. Focus less on the lack of delightfulness in getting started on your openness project and more on the delightful feelings of accomplishment as you move along.

10. *Use rational emotive imagery.* Practice without being there. Come to terms with the worst that could potentially happen in terms of outcome and discomfort. Close your eyes and picture yourself coming out of your cocoon by rendering opinions and suggestions. Vividly imagine failing to express yourself adequately, others strongly disapproving, and feeling a high amount of emotional upset - that is, shame, anxiety about being in this awkward social situation and feeling the way you do. Make the discomfort and disturbance feel worse; amplify it as if it were going out of style. Then, in the next breath, tone down your initial overreaction while continuing to imagine the same disappointing scene. Substitute a different emotion, such as regret, disappointment, or concern by forcing yourself to think differently about the same situation. Daily practice this coping tool designed to help you to touch all bases regarding your ability to better tolerate and accept the worst of all possible negative outcomes.

11. *No self-beratement.* Often people who act nonassertively will put themselves down following their error. Avoid this self-criticism trap by acknowledging your shortcoming and pledging to do better in the future, but minus the condemnation in the present.

12. *Establish a rational debate with yourself.* Contrasted thinking invites contrasting emotions and behaviors. Study, practice, and act upon the following strategy that

is designed to help challenge thoughts that are against your best emotional interests. When arguing against your irrational beliefs, monitor the tone of your voice so as to place stronger emphasis on the rational side of the debate ledger. Not only watch your language but listen to the strength of it. Not only debate against the irrational, but do so like you mean it!

IRRATIONAL IDEAS	COUNTERING RATIONAL IDEAS
"I can't say what is on my mind."	"I often won't say what is on my mind, but that doesn't mean I'm helpless to do so!"
"Every time I try to speak up I manage to say the wrong thing."	"I sometimes put my foot in my mouth, but I have no way of knowing ahead of time the outcome of my expressions."
"I couldn't stand looking like a horse's ass in front of everybody."	"I can stand anything as long as I'm alive, and I doubt whether saying the wrong thing will kill me. Besides, I'll never be a horse's ass - only a human being who sometimes acts asininely."
"If I state my piece, others may conflict with my ideas, and conflict, because it is unbearable, is to be avoided at all costs."	"True, others might openly disagree with my statements. False, that such differences are beyond the realm of toleration or are to be avoided under any circumstances."
"Humility is sacred. It would be terrible if, after hearing me out, others thought I was trying to show I was superior to them."	"Having a humble image is not all important or in many cases even desirable. Although it would be disappointing if others read my motives wrong, I wouldn't have to let such misunderstanding ruin my day."
"I have to know the perfect time, place, and manner to deliver my message, because if I don't do it just perfectly so, I'll be perfectly worthless."	"He who hesitates is lost. Besides, there is no such animal as perfect. Trying to find one is like trying to find a corner in a silo."

IRRATIONAL IDEAS *(Cont'd)*	COUNTERING RATIONAL IDEAS *(Cont'd)*
"I have to feel comfortable before I exercise my opinionated jaws. I shouldn't have to go through feeling out of sorts in order to say what is on my mind."	"Does it say on my birth certificate that I was born into the world to feel comfortable? I doubt it! I can voice my views and make feeling comfortable about it have nothing to do with the price of eggs."
"How shameful it would be to put myself out on a limb with my opinions only to have it fall off."	"Giving myself shame is for the birds! Such emotional baggage I can and plan to do without!"
"If I perform badly in expressing myself I would have to put myself down."	"If I perform badly I can put my performance down without putting myself down. In fact, putting myself down is never required."
"If others laugh at my opinions or even silently smirk at or politely disapprove of them, I could never face the world again."	"How well others handle or how much others approve of my notions does not have to be made to be tied in with my ability to deal with my world or anything in it."
"I shouldn't have to go through all the effort to form my opinions without a guarantee that they won't fall on deaf ears."	"Naturally, I'd like to be able to pick my spots in conversation knowing that my ideas will fall on receptive ears. However, there is no way in Hades that I can know others' agreeing response for tomorrow today."
"Correct, if I come up with good ideas others may continue to expect me to provide solutions to their future problems."	"Incorrect, that I would have to put undue pressure on myself about what others expect of me or that I am sworn to meet others' expectations."
"It's not like me to say what is on my mind, and I must not act out of character."	"The fact that I'm unaccustomed to voicing my thoughts doesn't mean that I cannot start doing so now. After all, there is no law of the universe to the contrary."

IRRATIONAL IDEAS *(Cont'd)*	COUNTERING RATIONAL IDEAS *(Cont'd)*
"The possibility that I could stumble and say the wrong thing that would meet with others' disapproval means I have to keep worrying and brooding about such a worst possible occurrence."	"Though in speaking my mind I could experience others' disdain, that doesn't mean I have to make myself lose sleep about that possibility. After all, worrying does not possess any magical qualities that will prevent bad things from happening."

Whatever you do, don't emotionally box yourself in like the client who explained that he was reluctant to voice his opinions for fear of group censure. Yet, he was also concerned about suffering in silence, for fear that his social group might deem him conceited in his quietude. Avoid such a "damned if you do and damned if you don't" double bind by deciding what you want to express or not express and resolving not to cause yourself suffering in either case. If you decide to open up, do so because you believe it would be in your best interest to. Don't overconcern yourself about whether you come across in acceptable fashion. Likewise, if you choose not to go public with your ideas, don't put undue pressure on yourself about what others might make of your silence. See that your life doesn't depend on outcome in either case.

Life isn't the dugout. Give strong consideration to putting yourself in the game. Don't hide your light under a bushel. See the light and put your best foot forward or others will miss the best of your contributions and you will miss the satisfactions of contributing. Don't act like you don't know what you do know. Instead, unmask and affirm your resources so that self and other profit can be intelligently revealed.

Pacifying Your Own Discomfort
By Suggesting That Others
Squelch Theirs

A 5-year-old child fell on the playground blacktop, skinning and bloodying his knee. As he tearfully approached the teacher with his pain, the teacher said, "Don't cry, it doesn't hurt." Discomfort anxiety is a term used to explain people's discomfort with their own anxiety. Having a hard time coping with their original discomfort, they startle themselves about it, insist that it immediately vanish, and in the process of this overreaction to the symptom of anxiety, they give themselves a multiplying emotional effect: double trouble, or anxiety about their anxiety This guide describes a similar yet different brand of discomfort anxiety: discomfort about someone else's discomfort. It will include rational ideas on how such discomforts can be less fearfully managed and what else can be done to better cope with another's pain to the benefit of both parties.

Feeling out of sorts about another's emotional pain has its roots in other pity - feeling sorry for someone else about that person's emotional upset. Empathy, having feelings about an associate's emotional discomfort, is carried to excess when such regret is exaggerated. The observers convince themselves that they just cannot bear the mark of others' pain. Because they view others' unhappiness as causing their own, they insist that the only way to stop feeling out of joint is for the others to find happiness or pretend that they are happy. "Deny your feelings so I can feel better" is the request of the observer. "I feel so uncomfortable when faced with your emotional pain, so would you please squelch it so that I can more pleasantly get on with my life?" is the observer's plea. The implication here is that because the observers believe that their discomfort is being caused by the others' upset, the observers are dependent on the others to invalidate or deny their feelings before the observers can feel better.

This sets the stage for anger. After all, if your discomfort is creating mine, and if you don't shut down your pain quickly, you're continuing to cause my suffering. Making yourself dependent on others to change before you can feel better, holding them accountable for your discomfort, is a real breeding ground and battleground for anger and resentment. Following are examples of demands for others to sweep their feelings under the rug and the anger that can be produced when the hurtful one is unable to abruptly switch emotional gears:

- *Situation 1.* A teenager tearfully informs his parents that his first love has decided to forsake him. The parents, feeling sorry for him and having difficulty tolerating their own sorrow for him, abruptly tell him, "Don't feel bad, there are a lot more fishes in the stream."

- *Situation 2.* A volunteer who is tired and overworked tells her paid supervisor of her lethargy. The supervisor, after making himself feel guilty for assigning so much work for this individual, tries to perfume guilt by quickly suggesting, "Don't worry, you'll feel better tomorrow, and I'll see to it that this never happens again."

- *Situation 3.* A mother who works both in and out of the home informs her mate that she is feeling emotionally and physically drained from her double responsibilities. Her partner tries to cover for his feelings of guilt and shame by suggesting that she quickly stop complaining and states, "It's not that bad, is it, I work hard too, don't forget."

- *Situation 4.* A student complains to his teacher that recent assignments given to him leave him with little time to do other things. Believing that her authority is being threatened, and making herself feel threatened about that, in an effort to distract herself from her insecurity she abruptly blurts out, "Other teachers expect even more than I do, so you don't have it as bad as you think."

- *Situation 5.* A teacher is told by a child, "I can't do multiplication tables." The teacher, feeling uneasy about her teaching abilities and in an effort to discard her discomfort, retorts, "Don't be silly, you can too learn multiplication tables, everyone else does."

- *Situation 6.* A public servant voices to a constituent that he is weary from long hours of working on a community project. The voter feels uneasy that he hasn't been offering assistance and replies, "If you don't like the heat, you can always get out of the kitchen."

- *Situation 7.* A coach explains to an alumnus that she is worried because she was just informed that her star player will be lost for the season. The alumnus, feeling put on the spot and uneasy himself, comments, "Never fear, good teams always rise to a higher level when under adversity."

- *Situation 8.* An associate explains to a friend his nervousness about an upcoming public presentation that he is required to give. Overidentifying with being in the public spotlight, and in an effort to appease his own emotional shivering, the friend states, "Don't be so anxious; you will do just fine. There is nothing for you to be concerned about."

All these examples illustrate the common insistency, "Convenience my comfort by overlooking your own." What can be done to avoid falling into this comfort trap where you seek a denial of another's feelings so that you can better tolerate your own? The following suggestions are in order for dealing with your own anxiety about someone else's discomfort:

1. *Use discomfort-reducing coping ideas.* The following portable one-liners can be quickly self-administered in order to interrupt other-pity symptoms about another's symptoms:

   • "I am not responsible for others' discomforts and upsets."
   • "I can well tolerate while nicely not exaggerating the significance of others' discomforts and upsets."
   • "Bear down against your low tolerance for frustration and bear with observing others' pain."
   • "I am not doing anyone any favors by hanging my hat on their upsets."
   • "If I pain myself about another's discomfort, I needlessly cause myself suffering - life is too short for that."
   • "I'd best not sanctify the avoidance of others' discomfort."
   • "I do not have to make myself dependent upon another's comfort."
   • "Others' discomfort is a part of life, but not bigger than life."
   • "I'd better not steam myself about others' queasiness, because that would only cook my own goose."
   • "I can well acclimate myself to others' undue discomfort, because when I don't, I cause myself undue fretfulness."
   • "Don't startle yourself about another's unwanted feelings, because that will only distract you from coping with your own."

- "If you brood about the discomforts of those whom you care for, you will likely end up resenting those whom you have brooded about."
- "A sense of humility may be all it would take to not bring my moods down about others' disadvantages. There are certain things that I can't do for others, including pushing their feelings out of their mind for them."

2. *Appreciate the lack of abruptness in human emotion.* Feelings cannot be turned off and on like a light switch. They can only be dimmed, gradually, over time, and only by the owner of them.

3. *Distinguish being disturbed about from being disturbed by.* See that the other's discomfort doesn't cause your upset but that you disturb yourself by your overreaction to it.

4. *Develop a philosophy of pain comparable with mental health.* Recognize that humans aren't in the world to feel never-ending comfort, but rather to experience the world, and that includes a fair amount of discomfort.

5. *Understand that free will swings both ways.* Just as your associate has a choice whether to overreact or not to overreact, so too do you have such a choice in reference to his or her original upset.

6. *Use three little words.* In an effort to actively understand the other and to offer yourself some protection from the other's discomforts, offer consolation with "I understand you." Rather than try to pull teeth by changing another's feelings, offer a sincere and thorough understanding of them, for example, "It sounds like you have some troublesome feelings about the matter."

7. *Own up to a sense of humility.* Come down off your high horse and accept the fact that you can't displace emotional pain from and transplant pleasure to another person.

8. *"What do you think" versus "don't you think."* Ask, don't tell. Ask what the other's thoughts are on the matter of concern, don't spoon-feed him or her quick fix solutions. That way he or she will be more likely to come up with his or her own answers, in his or her own time - without borrowing emotions from your pity.

9. *Appreciate individual differences.* Be sensitive to the fact that another person views and interprets the world through different peepers than you. As a result, it's understandable that the other takes his or her problems more seriously than you would and would like him or her to.

10. *Admit advice as easier to give than to follow.* By owning up to the fact that your infinite wisdom is likely to fall on deaf ears, and after all that you have said there is likely to be much more said than done, you will be better able to prompt restraint and not get yourself caught up in others' discomforts.

11. *Put forth a decent respect for human limitations.* Leading with the idea that your associate is limited in his or her ability to control his or her emotional anguish can help you to avoid getting yourself embroiled in his or her uncharted emotions. More fully appreciate how natural it is for him or her to feel and act in his or her agonizing ways so as to prevent your own agony.

12. *Be sensitive to others' rights to expression in all the wrong ways.* Though they may be wrong in their manner of expression by your book, explain to yourself that they are not answerable to you in doing so.

13. *Check if your overreaction is part of a more general problem.* Explore the possibility that you upset yourself about others' discomforts in similar ways that you upset yourself in other areas of your life; for example, your tendency to exaggerate the significance of events. That being the case, use your problem in coping with others' discomforts to work on your general mental health.

See that although it is natural to want to relieve yourself from emotional discomfort, try not to do so at another's expense. Instead, work on increasing your own tolerance for such unpleasantries. See your underlying message - "Don't cry, it doesn't hurt" - for what it is. Take the request-to-be-pacified words out of your mouth and replace them with more tolerant views and self-suggestions that will permit you to wean yourself from your cries for comfort. It is suggested that this will result in you doing more your own work for yourself and less trying the impossible of doing someone else's emotional self-management work for him or her.

Note. From *Feeling Right When Things Go Wrong* by Bill Borcherdt. Copyright © 1998, Professional Resource Exchange, Inc., P.O. Box 15560, Sarasota, FL 34277-1560.

GUIDE 30

Free Will, Human Limits, Rights to Be Wrong: Explaining the Seemingly Unexplainable

"How can he or she be that way?" This cry of frustration is often given when one party in a relationship acts badly and the others make themselves feel aghast about not being able to understand the simple reasons behind their associate's ill-advised conduct. The obvious but yet not-so-obvious answer is "EASILY!" How else would one expect a free-willed, limited, democratic member of society to act? According to your will, beyond their limits, according to carved-in-granite, fascist principles? I doubt it!

Understanding and accepting the following realities that are plain as the nose on your face will allow you to lighten the emotional load that comes from protesting against the way others naturally are, while using heavy doses of tolerance and acceptance to better lubricate contacts with them. The human givens I refer to are:

1. *Free will.* Humans have the freedom to direct their brain in the direction they want to, not in the direction that you want them to. Because of their free-thinking option, they don't have to have any special reasons to betray your value system. Decisions made are their choice - not your choice.

2. *Human limitations.* The sky is not the limit in terms of human potential. If your obnoxious-acting companions didn't have legs, you wouldn't expect them to walk. Likewise, if they are limited by their current emotional disturbance, what would be the point of demanding that they extend themselves beyond such a handicap?
3. *Rights to be wrong.* To say that humans don't have a right to be wrong is to say that they don't have a right to be human; that they are to be superhuman.

Accepting these major aspects of the human condition may seem like exceptionally bitter pills to swallow, but they will likely strengthen your gut on the way down - so take your medicine today and feel better tomorrow, rather than anguish yourself and feel worse for the rest of your life. The following method of bending your thinking rather than trying to bend the other may assist in not getting yourself bent out of shape when faced with another's negative actions. The rational debate format takes issue with the matter of intolerantly insisting that your fellow family or group member behave in a way that is more becoming to your values.

IRRATIONAL BELIEF	RATIONAL COUNTER
"He has no right to act in such dastardly ways - especially when it interferes with my conveniences."	"I'd best gracefully lump the fact that this or any other individual can thwart or balk me at their choosing."
"No one should act as foolish as she; what a babbling fool she is."	"She can exercise her right to act as foolish as she wishes, yet her conduct, as foolish as it is, does not constitute her as a fool."
"He had best explain, justify, and apologize for his antics, and he is to be condemned as a louse until he does."	"Since I am not (yet) the Lord God Almighty, this or any other person is not answerable to me."

IRRATIONAL BELIEF *(Cont'd)*	RATIONAL COUNTER *(Cont'd)*
"She could act better, and therefore she should; I could not tolerate such reprehensible behavior again."	"Even if she could act better, it wouldn't mean that she had to. Until she chooses to better her conduct, if and when she does, I can stand what I don't like about her oppositional conduct."
"What a wretch he is for acting more wretchedly than anyone should be allowed to."	"People choose to act wretchedly; no one allows them to. Better that I judge their wretched behavior without judging them."

Undamningly accept the way that others are by convincing yourself, "Isn't it unfortunate, but not horrible, that humans will likely continue to act the way they act, according to their free will, limitations, and rights to be wrong? Now how can I, as a flawed human being myself, better protect and get myself less upset about such wayward actions, preferably without condemning another as the sender or myself as the receiver of such negative tidings?" Such tolerant, accepting ideas have advantages of fuller emotional well-being.

Like it or not, others' nature dictates their actions, so you'd best not play dictator in trying to do it for them. Others do not stand on trial under your judgment. They don't have to explain themselves or undo your confusion about their actions. Better that you abolish your own uncertainty by accepting simple explanations to what at first sight seems to be unexplainable.

Note. From *Feeling Right When Things Go Wrong* by Bill Borcherdt. Copyright © 1998, Professional Resource Exchange, Inc., P.O. Box 15560, Sarasota, FL 34277-1560.

Bibliography

Alberti, R. E. (1990). *Stand Up, Speak Out, Talk Back.* San Luis Obispo, CA: Impact.

Alberti, R. E., & Emmons, M. L. (1975). *Stand Up, Speak Out, Talk Back!* New York: Pocket Books.

Alberti, R. E., & Emmons, M. L. (1990). *Your Perfect Right: A Guide to Assertive Living* (6th ed.). San Luis Obispo, CA: Impact.

Bach, G. R., & Wyden, P. (1968). *The Intimate Enemy.* New York: Avon.

Becker, W. C. (1971). *Parents Are Teachers.* Champaign, IL: Research Press.

Bell, N. W., & Vogel, E. F. (1965). *The Family.* New York: The Free Press.

Bernard, M. E., & Joyce, M. R. (1984). *Rational-Emotive Therapy With Children and Adolescents.* New York: John Wiley and Sons.

Borcherdt, B. (1989). *Think Straight! Feel Great! 21 Guides to Emotional Self-Control.* Sarasota, FL: Professional Resource Exchange.

Borcherdt, B. (1993). *You Can Control Your Feelings: 24 Guides to Emotional Well-Being.* Sarasota, FL: Professional Resource Press.

Borcherdt, B. (1996a). *Head Over Heart in Love: 25 Guides to Rational Passion.* Sarasota, FL: Professional Resource Press.

Borcherdt, B. (1996b). *Fundamentals of Cognitive-Behavior Therapy: From Both Sides of the Desk.* New York: Haworth Press.

245

Borcherdt, B. (1996c). *Making Families Work and What to Do When They Don't*. New York: Haworth Press.

Buntman, P. H. (1979). *How to Live With Your Teen-Ager*. Pasadena, CA: The Birch Tree Press.

Dobson, J. (1970). *Dare to Discipline*. New York: Bantam Books.

Dryden, W. (1990). *Dealing With Anger Problems: Rational-Emotive Therapeutic Interventions*. Sarasota, FL: Professional Resource Exchange.

Dryden, W. (1991). *A Dialogue With Albert Ellis: Against Dogma*. Philadelphia, PA: Open University Press.

Dryden, W., & DiGiuseppe, R. (1990). *A Primer on Rational-Emotive Therapy*. San Jose, CA: Resource Press.

Dryden, W., & Golden, W. L. (1987). *Cognitive-Behavioral Approaches to Psychotherapy*. Bristol, PA: Hemisphere Publishing.

Ellis, A. (1961). *A Guide to a Successful Marriage*. N. Hollywood, CA: Wilshire Book Company.

Ellis, A. (1965). *Suppressed: 7 Key Essays Publishers Dared Not Print*. Chicago, IL: New Classics House.

Ellis, A. (1966a). *The Art and Science of Love*. Secaucus, NJ: Lyle Stuart.

Ellis, A. (1966b). *How to Raise an Emotionally Healthy, Happy Child*. N. Hollywood, CA: Wilshire Book Company.

Ellis, A. (1971). *Growth Through Reason*. N. Hollywood, CA: Wilshire Book Company.

Ellis, A. (1972a). *The Civilized Couples Guide to Extra-Marital Affairs*. New York: Peter H. Wyden.

Ellis, A. (1972b). *The Sensuous Person: Critique and Corrections*. Secaucus, NJ: Lyle Stuart.

Ellis, A. (1974). *Humanistic Psychotherapy*. New York: McGraw-Hill.

Ellis, A. (1975). *How to Live With a Neurotic at Home and Work*. New York: Crown Publishers.

Ellis, A. (1979a). *The Intelligent Woman's Guide to Dating and Mating.* Secaucus, NJ: Lyle Stuart.

Ellis, A. (1979b). *Overcoming Procrastination.* New York: Signet.

Ellis, A. (1979c). *Reason and Emotion in Psychotherapy.* Secaucus, NJ: The Citadel Press.

Ellis, A. (1982). *Rational Assertiveness Training* (Audiotape). New York: Institute for Rational Living.

Ellis, A. (1988). *How to Stubbornly Refuse to Make Yourself Miserable About Anything--Yes, Anything!* Secaucus, NJ: Lyle Stuart.

Ellis, A. (1991). *Why Am I Always Broke: How to be Sure about Money.* New York: Carol Publishing.

Ellis, A., & Abrahms, E. (1978). *Brief Psychotherapy in Medical and Health Practice.* New York: Springer.

Ellis, A., & Becker, I. (1982). *A Guide to Personal Happiness.* N. Hollywood, CA: Wilshire Book Company.

Ellis, A., & Harper, R. (1975). *A New Guide to Rational Living.* N. Hollywood, CA: Wilshire Book Company.

Ellis, A., & Whiteley, J. (1979). *Theoretical and Empirical Foundation of Rational-Emotive Therapy.* Monterey, CA: Brooks/Cole.

Ellis, A., & Yeager, R. J. (1989). *Why Some Therapies Don't Work: The Dangers of Transpersonal Psychology.* Buffalo, NY: Prometheus Books.

Fensterheim, H., & Baer, J. (1977). *Don't Say Yes When You Want to Say No.* New York: Dell.

Fraiberg, S. H. (1959). *The Magic Years.* New York: Charles Scribner's Sons.

Frankl, V. E. (1959). *Man's Search for Meaning.* New York: Touchstone Books.

Garcia, E. (1979). *Developing Emotional Muscle.* Atlanta: Author.

Garner, A. (1981). *Conversationally Speaking.* New York: McGraw-Hill.

Glasser, W. (1975). *Reality Therapy*. New York: Harper Colophon Books.

Greenberg, D. (1966). *How to Make Yourself Miserable*. New York: Random House.

Greiger, R. M., & Boyd, J. D. (1980). *Rational-Emotive Therapy: A Skills Based Approach*. New York: Van Nostrand Reinhold.

Grossack, M. (1976). *Love, Sex, and Self-Fulfillment*. New York: Signet.

Haley, J., & Hoffman, L. (1967). *Techniques of Family Therapy*. New York: Basic Books.

Harris, S. (1982). *Pieces of Eight*. Boston: Houghton Mifflin.

Hauck, P. (1971). *Marriage Is a Loving Business*. Philadelphia, PA: The Westminster Press.

Hauck, P. (1974). *Overcoming Frustration and Anger*. Philadelphia, PA: The Westminster Press.

Hauck, P. (1976). *How to Do What You Want to Do*. Philadelphia, PA: The Westminster Press.

Hauck, P. (1978). *Overcoming Depression*. Philadelphia, PA: The Westminster Press.

Hauck, P. (1981). *Overcoming Jealousy and Possessiveness*. Philadelphia, PA: The Westminster Press.

Hauck, P. (1984). *The Three Faces of Love*. Philadelphia, PA: The Westminster Press.

Hoffer, E. (1966). *The True Believer*. New York: Perennial Library.

Holt, J. (1970a). *How Children Fail*. New York: Dell.

Holt, J. (1970b). *How Children Learn*. New York: Dell.

James, M., & Jongeward, D. (1973). *Born to Win*. Reading, PA: Addison-Wesley.

Johnson, W. R. (1981). *So Desperate the Fight*. New York: Institute for Rational Living.

Jourard, S. (1971). *The Transparent Self*. New York: D. Van Nostrand.

Lazarus, A. A. (1981). *The Practice of Multi-Modal Therapy.* New York: McGraw-Hill.

Lazarus, A. A. (1984). *In the Minds Eye: The Power of Imagery for Personal Enrichment.* New York: Guilford.

Lazarus, A. A. (1985). *Marital Myths: Two Dozen Mistaken Beliefs That Can Ruin a Marriage (or Make a Bad One Worse).* San Luis Obispo, CA: Impact.

Lazarus, A. A. (1989). *The Practice of Multimodal Therapy: Systematic, Comprehensive and Effective Psychotherapy.* Johns Hopkins.

Lazarus, A. A., & Fay, A. (1975). *I Can If I Want to.* New York: Warner Books.

Maultsby, M. (1975). *Help Yourself to Happiness.* New York: Institute for Rational Living.

Meichenbaum, D. (1977). *Cognitive-Behavior Modification: An Integrative Approach.* New York: Plenum.

Paris, C., & Casey, B. (1979). *Project: You, a Manual of Rational Assertiveness Training.* Portland, OR: Bridges Press.

Paterson, G. R. (1978). *Families.* Champaign, IL: Research Press.

Perls, F. S. (1969). *In and Out of the Garbage Pail.* New York: Bantam Books.

Putney, S., & Putney, G. J. (1966). *The Adjusted American: Normal Neuroses in the Individual and Society.* New York: Harper Colophon Books.

Reisman, D. (1962). *The Lonely Crowd.* New Haven: Yale University Press.

Russell, B. (1971). *The Conquest of Happiness.* New York: Liveright.

Russianoff, P. (1983). *Why Do I Think I'm Nothing Without a Man?* New York: Bantam Books.

Satir, V. (1967). *Conjoint Family Therapy.* Palo Alto, CA: Science and Behavior Books.

Satir, V. (1972). *Peoplemaking.* Palo Alto, CA: Science and Behavior Books.

Shedd, C. W. (1978). *Smart Dads I Know.* New York: Avon.

Simon, S. B. (1978). *Negative Criticism and What You Can Do About It.* Niles, IL: Argus Communications.

Smith, M. J. (1975). *When I Say No, I Feel Guilty.* New York: Bantam Books.

Walen, S. R., DiGiuseppe, R., & Wessler, R. L. (1980). *A Practitioner's Guide to Rational-Emotive Therapy.* New York: Oxford University Press.

Weeks, C. (1981). *Simple, Effective Treatment of Agoraphobia.* New York: Bantam Books.

Young, H. S. (1974). *A Rational Counseling Primer.* New York: Institute for Rational Living.

Zilbergeld, B. (1978). *Male Sexuality.* Boston, MA: Little, Brown, and Company.

Zilbergeld, B. (1983). *The Shrinking of America: Myths of Psychological Change.* Boston, MA: Little, Brown, and Company.

Zilbergeld, B. (1992). *The New Male Sexuality.* New York: Bantam Books.

Zilbergeld, B., & Lazarus, A. A. (1988). *Mindpower: Getting What You Want Through Mental Training.* New York: Ivy Books.

If You Found This Book Useful . . .

You might want to know more about our other titles.

If you would like to receive our latest catalog, please return this form:

Name:_____
(Please Print)

Address:_____

Address:_____

City/State/Zip:_____
This is ☐ home ☐ office

Telephone:(_____)_____

I am a:

_____ Psychologist
_____ Psychiatrist
_____ School Psychologist
_____ Clinical Social Worker

_____ Mental Health Counselor
_____ Marriage and Family Therapist
_____ Not in Mental Health Field
_____ Other:_____

◆   ◆   ◆

Professional Resource Press
P.O. Box 15560
Sarasota, FL 34277-1560

Telephone #800-443-3364
FAX #941-343-9201
E-mail at mail@prpress.com

FR/9/98

Add A Colleague To Our Mailing List . . .

If you would like us to send our latest catalog to one of your colleagues, please return this form.

Name:_____
                          (Please Print)

Address:_____

Address:_____

City/State/Zip:_____
                    This is ☐ home ☐ office

Telephone:(_____)_____

This person is a:

_____ Psychologist   _____ Mental Health Counselor
_____ Psychiatrist   _____ Marriage and Family Therapist
_____ School Psychologist   _____ Not in Mental Health Field
_____ Clinical Social Worker _____ Other:_____

Name of person completing this form:_____

◆   ◆   ◆

**Professional Resource Press
P.O. Box 15560
Sarasota, FL 34277-1560**

**Telephone #800-443-3364
FAX #941-343-9201
E-mail at mail@prpress.com**

FR/9/98